CONTENTS

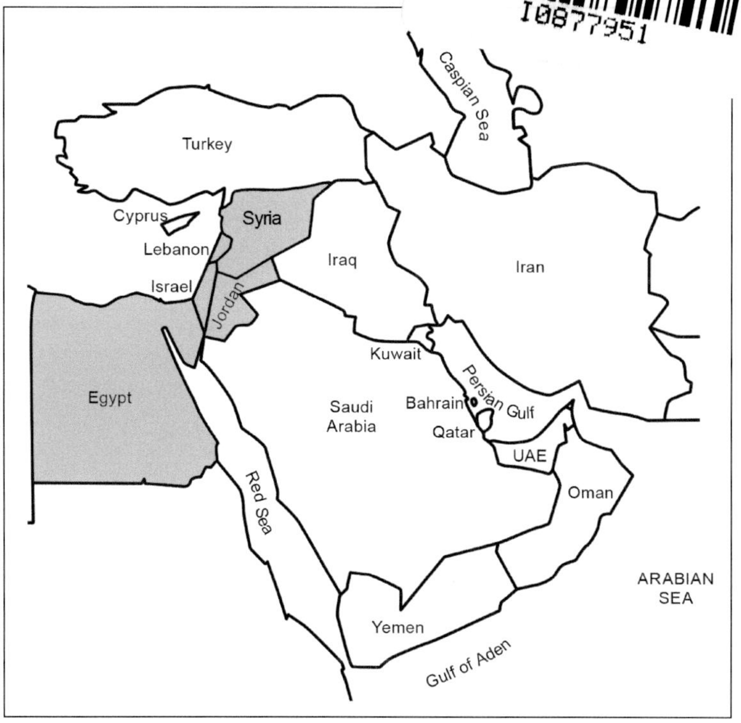

NOTE

In order to simplify the use of this book, all names, locations and geographic designations are as provided in *The Times World Atlas*, or other traditionally accepted major sources of reference, as of the time of described events. Similarly, Arabic names are romanised and transcripted rather than transliterated. For example: the definite article al- before words starting with 'sun letters' is given as pronounced instead of simply as al- (which is the usual practice for non-Arabic speakers in most English-language literature and media). For the reasons of space, ranges – which are usually measured in feet and nautical miles in international aeronautics – are cited in metric measurements with English units in parenthesis.

COVER

The most numerous attack jet in the Arab air forces facing Israel in 1967–1973 was the Mikoyan-Gurevich MiG-17F. It was a gravely dated warplane by this time with poor avionics, deficient range and modest payload. Yet, the fighter pilots bravely flew them on strike missions, especially Egyptians penetrating Israeli defences in western Sinai, as seen in this low flying example passing a United Nations vehicle. UARAF serial 2034, shown in the profile, displays the common colours and markings of the period 1968–1969. (Artwork by Tom Cooper)

Helion & Company Limited
Unit 8 Amherst Business Centre, Budbrooke Road, Warwick CV34 5WE, England
Tel. 01926 499 619
Email: info@helion.co.uk Website: www.helion.co.uk Twitter: @helionbooks Visit our blog http://blog.helion.co.uk/

Published by Helion & Company 2022
Designed and typeset by Mach 3 Solutions Ltd (www.mach3solutions.co.uk)
Cover designed by Paul Hewitt, Battlefield Design (www.battlefield-design.co.uk)

ISBN 978-1-804512-25-8

British Library Cataloguing-in-Publication Data.
A catalogue record for this book is available from the British Library.

For details of other military history titles published by Helion & Company Limited contact the above address, or visit our website: http://www.helion.co.uk. We always welcome receiving book proposals from prospective authors.

ACRONYMS AND ABBREVIATIONS

AAA	antiaircraft artillery
AAM	air-to-air missile
AB	Air Base
ADC	Air Defence Command
a.k.a.	also known as
APC	armoured personnel carrier
AR	aerial refuelling
ARM	anti-radiation missile
cal	calibre
COIN	counter-insurgency
COMINT	communications intelligence
ECCM	electronic counter-countermeasures
ECM	electronic countermeasures
ELINT	electronic intelligence
ESM	electronic support countermeasures
EW	electronic warfare
FAC	fast attack craft
FAC(M)	fast attack craft - missile
FAL	Force Aérienne Libanaise (Lebanese Air Force)
ft	foot, feet
g	acceleration due to gravity
GCI	ground-control interception
HAS	hardened aircraft shelters
IAF	Israel Air Force
IAI	Israel Aircraft Industries
IAP	International Airport
IDF	Israel Defence Forces
IFF	identification friend-or-foe
IN	Israel Navy
INS	Israel Navy Ship
IR	infrared
kg	kilogramme(s)
km	kilometre(s)
lb	pound(s)
m	metre(s)
mi	statute mile, miles
mm	millimetre(s)
MoD	Ministry of Defence
MTB	motor torpedo boat
NATO	North Atlantic Treaty Organization
NCO	non-commissioned officer
nm	nautical mile(s)
OP	observation post
ORBAT	order-of-battle
PDLFP	Popular Democratic Front for the Liberation of Palestine
PFLP	Popular Front for the Liberation of Palestine
PFLP-GC	Popular Front for the Liberation of Palestine – General Command
PLA	Palestine Liberation Army
PLO	Palestine Liberation Organization
PM	Prime Minister
PR	photo-reconnaissance
PASC	Palestine Armed Struggle Command
recce	reconnaissance
RPG	rocket-propelled grenades
RJAF	Royal Jordanian Air Force
rpm	rounds per minute
RWR	radar warning receiver
SAM	surface-to-air missile
SEAD	suppression of enemy air defences
SIGINT	signals intelligence
SPG	self-propelled gun
specops	special operations
SSM	surface-to-surface missiles
SyAAF	Syrian Arab Air Force
UAR	United Arab Republic
UARAF	United Arab Republic Air Force
UN	United Nations
UNTSO	United Nations Truce Supervision Organization
USA, US	United States of America
USAF	United States Air Force
USSR	Union of Soviet Socialist Republics

FOREWORD AND ACKNOWLEDGEMENTS

Following the June 1967 Arab-Israeli War tensions on the new borders soon flared anew. All the involved militaries remained very active over the next six years with more consistent mobilisation, intensive training, and action than ever before. As the combat grew in scope, the cost escalated in lives, materiel, and treasure. Each side deepened their dependence on superpower arms supply and mediation. The geopolitical stakes rose and Israel found itself fighting the Soviets indirectly on the borders and terrorist internationally. Adversary forces grew in size, adopted more complex weapons, and trained in new tactics, all in the tumult of combat of escalating intensity. Fallout from the conflict affected all the Arab states given the acrimony, public desire to punish Israel, and guerrillas acting from national territory bringing Israeli retaliation. These factors were destabilising to varying degrees with Arab-on-Arab violence growing and a shift to more radical policies.

This period is collectively referred to as the War of Attrition. It was an extraordinary time of confrontation, irregular warfare, rising terrorism, and national struggles seldom seen before or since. It became the world's most violent, costly, and dangerous conflict after that in Southeast Asia. At the centre of it, Israel found herself engaged on all sides and isolated as never before. The struggle altered the geopolitical landscape and set the stage for the October 1973 Arab-Israeli War.

The named War of Attrition on the Suez Canal was begun by Egypt on 8 March 1969 and ended with a ceasefire 17 months later. While delving deeply into the 'eye of the hurricane', these volumes will examine the interlocking Arab-Israeli conflict across the entire period with all combatants. Arab-on-Arab violence and Palestinian internecine struggles, tangential 'fallout' of the Arab-Israeli conflict, are addressed only as far as they affected that broader conflict. No attempt is made to document every military action on all the fronts. Such would fill many books. Being a book on war, deep excursions into national politics are also avoided. Given that concurrent events on the separate fronts are discussed in separate volumes and chapters, a timeline is presented in the final volume to help the reader appreciate the scope of the broad conflict.

I am well aware of the lingering animus regarding these events, with aspects of the conflict persisting to the present day. I do not have any personal connection to the events or participants, then or now. I worked for an honest and impartial account avoiding stereotypes and loaded labels or phrases. That I would still offend was understood, but it is not intentional. Any errors of facts or interpretation are likewise unintentional.

I would like to thank E.R. (Ted) Hooton for his research on the Egyptian, Israeli, Jordanian and Syrian armies which is incorporated in this work.

Bill Norton (nortowj1@gmail.com)
Tehachapi, California, 2022

INTRODUCTION

The roots of the Arab-Israeli conflict lay in deep history. The Holly Land had swapped rulers several times over the centuries. Following the First World War the British acquired a mandate from the League of Nations to govern the area then known as Palestine. Demographically the people that would come to be known as Palestinians were largely Muslim and from various tribes collectively called Arabs. People from the Jewish diaspora began returning to Palestine with Zionist aspirations (to re-establish a Jewish homeland) and to escape persecution in Europe and elsewhere. After the Second World War and the Holocaust this migration turned into a flood of Jews that markedly shifted the cultural and racial makeup of Palestine. This was resisted by the Arab inhabitants with ever greater violence.

British efforts to control the situation became increasingly costly after the Second World War and she turned to the new United Nations (UN) for resolution. In November 1947 the UN voted to partition Palestine into Arab and Jewish nations. Israel declared its statehood on 14 May 1948, the day the Mandate ended. It was also the day war began as surrounding Arab countries moved to prevent what they saw as an injustice and to also grab portions of the land it believed the Jews could not defend. The resulting year-long war saw Israel defeat its foes and firmly establish itself. The 1949 boundaries were called the Green Line. Egypt held the Gaza Strip in the south under military administration adjacent to its Sinai region while Transjordan held the area in the east, which would come to be known as the West Bank of the Jordan River, which included the eastern portion of Jerusalem. The warring parties signed an armistice that established these frontiers based on the military situation while also agreeing to norms of behaviour regarding the boundaries. The Arabs would not negotiate peace treaties and so animosity between the parties persisted. During the war hundreds of thousands of Palestinians had fled or were evicted from the war zone into adjacent countries and then were denied return to their homes and property inside Israel. The UN establish dozens of refugee camps for these people in the West Bank, the renamed Jordan, Syria, the Gaza Strip, and Lebanon. The inhabitants were increasingly frustrated as years then decades passed with no hope for a solution to their plight. The Arab states generally declined to absorb these people as citizens for various reasons, one being to maintain a complaint against Israel's existence. Israel absorbed Jews expelled by Arab states plus more from around the world.

There were continuing low-level conflicts with shelling incidents from Egypt across the southern border, the Syrians from the Golan Heights overlooking Israel's Galilee region, and east from Jordan. Irregular warfare was sponsored by these states employing Palestinian recruits to harass Israel through sabotage and murder. The Israelis responded to the terrorism with reprisal raids and clandestine operations across the frontier in disproportion to the provocation as a means to instil restraint. This tit-for-tat violence was one motivation for Israel joining Great Britain and France in the October–November 1956 war against Egypt over President Gamal Abdel al-Nasser's nationalisation of the Suez Canal. The Anglo-French campaign was halted by international pressure, but Israel succeeded in seizing the entire Sinai Peninsula and the Gaza Strip. She had to withdraw months later under the terms of another armistice.

The charismatic Nasser's 'defeat' of the invaders raised his standing on the 'Arab Street' and he assumed a self-assigned role as the 'leader of the Arab world.'[1] As a tool of statecraft, he sustained animosity for Israel as a national and religious foe to draw his citizens around, in promoting pan-Arab nationalism, and while paying lip service to championing the stateless Palestinian aspirations. He also worked to gather surrounding nations in an alliance for mutual benefit and to confront Israel.[2] An arms race ensued in the 1950s and 1960s that posed a grave threat to Israel who could never hope to match the number of military personnel and materiel resources of the 'confrontation states.' Consequently, Israel adopted a strategy of pre-emption to attack its enemies first if war appeared imminent, ensuring opposition forces were reduced and combat was not waged on Israeli soil. The war would then be short before the UN and superpower nations imposed a ceasefire.

Israel was compelled to execute its pre-emption strategy in June 1967 then Nasser drew Jordan and Syria into an alliance that threatened to eradicate Israel. The resulting Six-Day War was an incredible success for Israel who defeated the opposing armies in one of the most astonishing and effective campaigns of modern warfare. The world marvelled at little Israel's resounding victory while the Arabs seethed. Israel occupied vast tracts of Arab land and additional Palestinians were displaced into surrounding countries. Termed 'The Setback' (*al-Naksah*), the defeat deeply shook the Arab world. They saw Western support for Israel as an extension of the colonialism they had suffered under, an effort to suppress rising Arab progressivism, and a continuing disregard for Arab rights and sensibilities.

The conflict appeared destined to continue. Israel was unlikely to compel its adversaries to negotiate a final peace settlement by force of arms. The Arab armies appeared to have little chance of eliminating Israel entirely and reclaiming lost territory via war. Negotiation was the most promising course of action, but the parties were far apart on their objectives, tainted by animosity. They made ready for further war. Always one of the world's more notorious lingering conflicts, the closing of the Suez Canal following the 1967 war moved the conflict to high priority on the international stage.

Displaced from their homes in Palestine, more Palestinian dislocations occurred from territories occupied by the IDF during the 1967 war. Here people are seen crossing the damaged Allenby Bridge spanning the Jordan River between the West Bank and Jordan. (Israel GPO)

These Zahal personnel examine the east bank span of the Firdan Bridge on the Suez Canal. Within weeks such would not be possible as Egyptian soldiers on the west bank would fire on anyone exposed across the waterway. Firdan, the largest metal swing bridge in the world at the time, would be largely destroyed in the coming combat. (Albert Grandolini collection)

The territory captured by Israel in the Six-Day War and subsequently occupied is depicted. Land boundaries to be defended were shorter than before the war but coastlines to be patrolled were longer. The occupation demanded much from the IDF and so the force grew and costs increased. More than a million Arab inhabitants dwelled in these 'administered' areas.

1

PICKING UP THE PIECES

The armed forces of Egypt, Syria and Jordan stood badly battered but uncowed following the war. They needed to reequip, reorganise, and retrain in preparing for any further engagement with Israel. Even beyond the confrontation states the war was cause for other Arab nations and Palestinian combatants to do the same. All vowed to regain both land and honour but recognised it would be a long, hard task. Arab nations assumed there would be more conflict and Egypt in particular intended to make war on Israel at the earliest opportunity. The Soviet Union was the principal source of their weapons, expanding its influence in the region. Israel, too, had to replace combat loses but also sought to modernise. Diplomats hunted for ways to bring the parties to peace negotiations and prevent another war.

EGYPTIAN REBUILDING

Egypt had the largest armed forces in the region and was the most influential within the Arab sphere. It was also the most badly mauled. When the Israel Defence Forces (IDF, or the acronym-derived Zahal) had finished with Egypt the heart of her armed forces had been torn out, both in materiel and morale. Perhaps 17 percent of its personnel were killed, captured, or deserted. Over 9,800 were dead or missing, including 1,500 officers. It also lost 85 percent of its equipment, the vast majority abandoned intact on the battlefield. This included 820 tanks and some 450 guns. Although 57,000 men and 115 tanks managed to return from Sinai, munitions were severely depleted and there was a bare minimum of forces between the ceasefire line on the Suez Canal and Cairo.

In Sinai thousands of UAR soldiers, abandoned by their officers, had left their weapons and equipment, shucked their boots, and began walking west over 160km (100mi) or more in the harsh desert. Hundreds died of thirst and hunger or fell prey to Bedouin marauders. The IDF rounded up some 5,000 of the men, provided them sustenance, and held them in prisoner-of-war (POW) camps.[1] Israel did seek to interrogate the officers, but these soon removed their rank insignia and blended in with the conscripts. Only when the Israelis learned that the officers wore silk shorts while the common soldier had cotton were they able to identify the officers by having captives drop their trousers![2] A POW exchange between Egypt and Israel occurred

Israel's surprise attack on the morning of 5 June 1967, and attacks throughout the day, destroyed most of Egypt's air force and then that of Syria and Jordan. This image helps convey both the damage done (two Il-14s and an Mi-6 destroyed) and the IAF's ability to conduct virtually unopposed photo-reconnaissance flights over surrounding states for a few months following (the shadow of the Vautour IIBR shooting the image also captured). (IAF)

Israel had collected thousands of Egyptian soldiers in Sinai and held them until January 1968 when an arranged POW exchanged occurred. These men are being transported to a holding centre for interrogation and processing. Such images did not sit well with the Arab public. (IDF Spokesman)

on 19 January 1968. Israel transported those it held to a handoff point in El Qantarah, on the east bank of the canal, where Egypt ferried them across. Once they were in Egypt-proper these personnel were kept in desert camps until 'reconditioned.' Some simply went home and took off their uniforms instead of returning to their barracks. It was the low point for the Egyptian Army. The regard for the armed forces in the public eye was one of derision and many servicemen were ashamed to wear their uniforms. Officers visiting their units were sometimes met with indifference by the non-commissioned officers (NCO).

The nation suffered a crisis of confidence in the whole of the Revolution and 'Arab Socialism.' Disquiet with the regime and the extent of the 1967 defeat prompted many in the military and the country at large to focus on religion and dedication to the state rather than Nasser's populism and cult of personality. The regime leveraged off this focus to help guide the morals of the soldiers.

The United Arab Republic Air Force (UARAF) had lost only 4 percent of its 20,000 personnel but 90 percent of its combat capability that included 72 percent of its fighter aircraft, all of its bombers, 28 percent of its helicopters, and 37 percent of its transports.[3] Remaining operable aircraft were flown to dispersal fields beyond the Israel Air Force's (IAF) reach, and those repairable followed by road transport. Of the 27 S-75 surface-to-air missiles (SAM) batteries (three brigades with more than 750 missiles, only half deployed in the 25 prepared sites), two had been lost in Sinai, at least two bombed west of the canal, and others near the canal moved out of artillery range of the IDF.[4] Vital radar stations were also lost in Sinai or bombed in the Nile Delta. Of its 15 principal airfields, the UARAF had lost the four in Sinai and the two along the east bank of the canal, within artillery range, had to be abandoned. The five bases in the delta were insufficient to host the squadrons required to defend the country.

Many in the Arab world were angry that the Union of Soviet Socialist Republics (USSR) had not immediately come to the aid of Arab combatants when Israel launched its offensive. Seeking to regain goodwill and make amends for promulgating erroneous intelligence that had helped spark the crisis, the Soviet Union moved promptly to shore-up its allies in the region. Within days of the war's end, President Nasser appealed to the USSR for assistance in rebuilding his army. He went further and asked the Kremlin for immediate air cover. This suggested a large-scale deployment of Soviet combat forces and equipment to Egypt. They demurred but threatened to intervene militarily if the Israelis crossed the canal, invading Egypt-proper. They further promised to rapidly replace all losses on a one-for-one basis and give Egypt priority on new weapons in the future, essentially co-equal with Warsaw Pact nations, to reverse the results of Israeli 'aggression.' All equipment at that time and for years following were provided either gratis or on exceedingly favourable financial terms. President Nikolai Podgorny came on 21 June for a summit with Nasser.

The Soviet Union initiated an enormous and rapid resupply effort. This was supervised by a delegation that began arriving on 16 June led by Chief of the General Staff and Deputy Defence Minister Marshal Matvei Vasilevich Zakharov. Arriving on the 20th, he spent a fortnight in the region. They assessed Egypt's requirements and then worked to help her assimilate the equipment. A military mission was formed under former Carpathian Military District commander Colonel General Petr Lashchenko and the air force's Lieutenant General Aleksandr Vybronov. This was followed on 26 June by a Czech mission. While the Egyptians clamoured for replacement and improved weapons, Zakharov was sceptical. 'Arms? What do you need more arms for? To deliver these to the Israelis too? What you need is training, training. Then we will see about arms.' Regardless, from 12 June the Soviet Union sent a stream of supplies delivered via a fleet of 20 An-12 transport airplanes, flying 544 sorties across 40 days, and 15 ships docked in Egyptian ports at a rate of two or three per week through mid-October. (The military airlifters were given commercial markings and aircrew wore civilian attire.) Delivered were 48,000 tonnes of equipment, spares and ammunition, some drawn from Warsaw Pact arsenals. Within a month 70 percent of Egypt's armed force's equipment had been restored and approximately full strength by the end of the year.[5] In Egypt, as elsewhere, the first tranche of Soviet equipment boosted the confidence of the armed forces. The USSR showed its commitment in another way on 3 December with a slow fly-over of Cairo by a formation of Soviet Air Forces Tu-16 bombers.

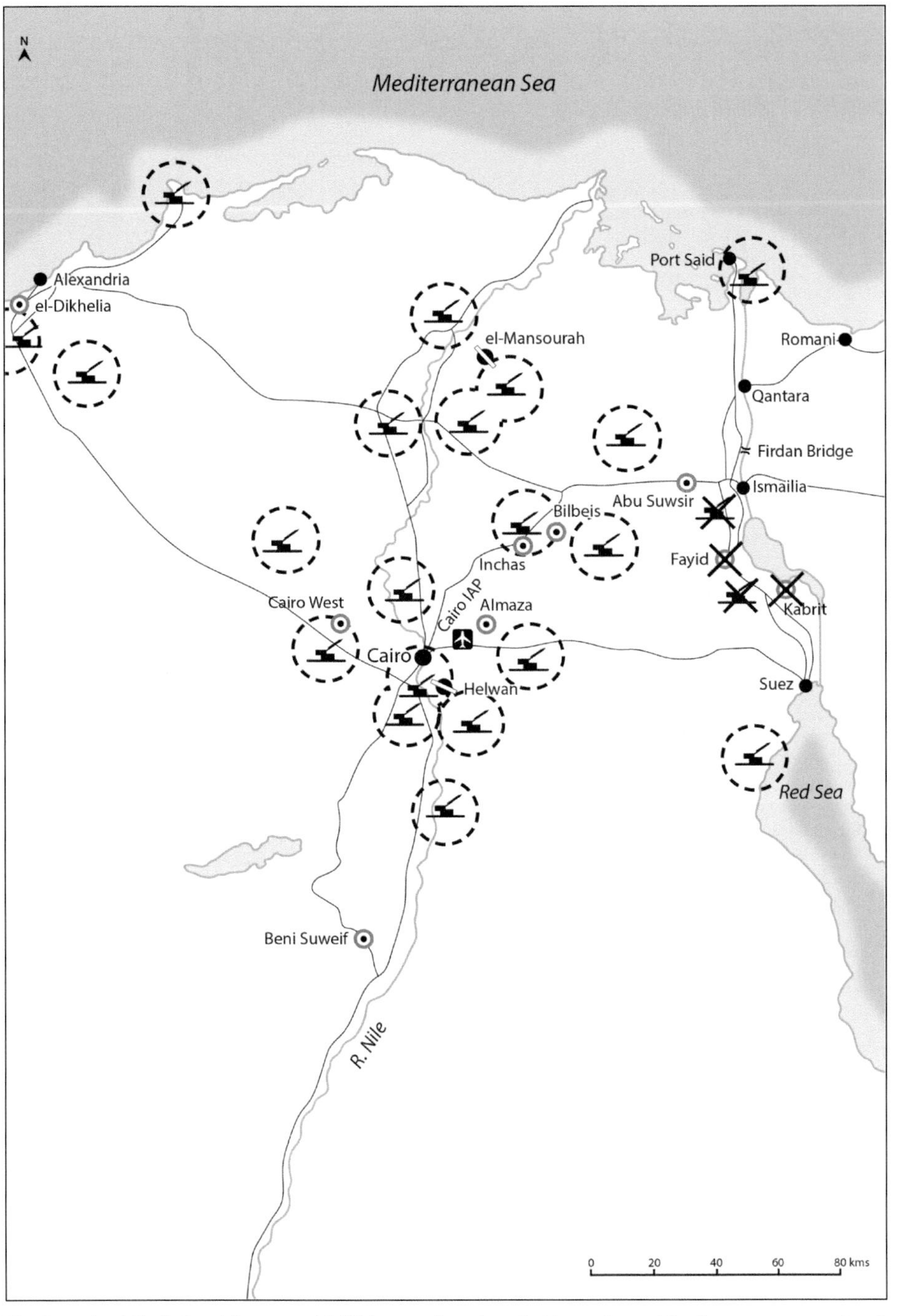

The Egyptian Nile Delta airbases and SAM battery locations (with medium altitude engagement rings) immediately following the Six-Day War are shown. The two S-75 batteries captured by the IDF in Sinai are not included while the two sites near the west bank are indicated as abandoned (along with Kabrit and Fayid ABs) as they fell within range of Israeli artillery. Four batteries around Aswan, farther south, are not depicted. There were then 25 prepared S-75 sites though not all initially housed a battery. (The map was derived from an IAF Intelligence Branch depiction of pre-war SAM dispositions.)

Deliveries included flown-in and crated combat aircraft from USSR and East European squadrons with 65 MiG-21s and 123 MiG-17s, 10 Su-7s, 10 Il-28s, 18 Tu-16s, and 10 Mi-8 helicopters (new to the UARAF). Aircraft were assembled by Soviet technicians so that squadron personnel could focus on mission readiness. Algeria lent 20 MiG-21s, 21 MiG-17Fs, 12 Su-7s (joining a dozen crated in Egypt and six from elsewhere), and 12 Il-28s to fill immediate needs. They were flown in by Egyptian pilots and apparently remained throughout the conflict. The MiG-19s had had such a poor record that the type was not refreshed following war losses. In Yemen, where the Egyptians were embroiled in the civil war, she gave a few aircraft to the Republican forces while at least 100 crated aircraft and eight Il-28s there were brought home. Hundreds of pilots and maintainers were sent to the USSR for retraining.

The USSR insisted on sending a large number of 'advisors' to supervise assimilation, training, and employment of the weapons. They asserted unprecedented supervision and even unit command. These were initially 100 officers but quickly expanded to approximately 1,500 military personnel (compared to 250 or so before the war). These were mostly junior officers but went up to Soviet and Czech general officers with Colonel General Lashchenko as chief advisor. (Lashchenko went home in November 1968 to become Deputy Commander-in-Chief of Ground Forces, relieved by Colonel General Ivan Katyshkin who remained until September 1970.) They manned some equipment as combat troops in order to buck-up defences straightaway but principally served as trainers and offered specialist technical assistance. Housing and wages were provided by the host. Egyptians disliked the presence of foreign military personnel given her colonial past but acknowledged the short-term necessity given the dire situation. Such massive movement of hardware and stationing of personnel outside Europe

A dour Marshal Andrei Grechko, USSR Minister of Defence, meets pilots during a visit to an Egyptian air base during 1969 accompanied by UARAF chief Air Vice Marshal Shalaby Hinnawi (right). The presence of Grechko and other senior Soviet civilian and military officials in Egypt emphasised the importance the USSR placed on restoring and supporting the Egyptian military and leadership. (Albert Grandolini collection)

Israeli PR imagery indicates the crated aircraft and unassembled MiG-21s collected at a UARAF airfield awaiting attention. The Soviet Union was generous in rapidly rearming its Arab associates, flying in especially warplanes aboard large An-12 transports and providing technicians to assemble the machines. In this way the air forces regained strength within months of their defeat, aided by the fact they had suffered only modest personnel loses. (IDF)

The MiG-19 was so problem-plagued that fleet losses in the war were not greatly grieved. The USSR did not provide replacements – nor were they sought. The UARAF employed those that remained strictly for training purposes – when they could be put into the air. (Tom Cooper collection)

The Il-28 was quite a dated jet bomber by 1967 yet the USSR supplied more as replacement for war losses. The Egyptian pilots bravely flew them into combat against the Israelis well aware of their vulnerability. (Albert Grandolini collection)

by the USSR was unprecedented and so closely watched by North Atlantic Treaty Organization (NATO) militaries.

Despite failing to prevent the defeat and the perceived failure of Soviet arms, the USSR retained and strengthened its position in the region. Its willingness to continue supporting Egypt and the other affected Arab states was of mutual benefit. Apart from demonstrating it stood by its associates, the USSR gained additional influence and basing for its military assets in the Mediterranean Sea facing NATO elements. President Nasser influenced Soviet assistance via the granting of port visits, using Cold War dynamics to his nation's advantage. Soon there was at least one Soviet vessel in Alexandria and Port Said harbours persistently as a means of discouraging Israeli attacks. In March 1968 the partners finalised a bilateral treaty conceding to the USSR significant basing privileges. The Soviet Navy soon established considerable presence in several ports with hundreds of personnel and large stores supporting its warships. Over the next year this brought a naval surveillance squadron with Tu-16Rs, Il-38 anti-submarine warfare aircraft, and Be-12 seaplanes operating from Alexandria and Mersa Matruh, all bearing Egyptian markings. The Soviets virtually took over Cairo West airport for their operations, coming and going without notice and sans customs inspections.

Moscow was determined to maintain a degree of control over the military situation in the region. Egyptian requests for sufficient equipment to regain the Sinai Peninsula were politely brushed aside because the Soviets felt their over-eager Arab comrades were still incapable of making the best use of the material they had already received. The USSR did not relish another potential defeat of its regional allies, and its own loss of prestige, via premature combat and the optics of ineffective Soviet arms. Hence, she became

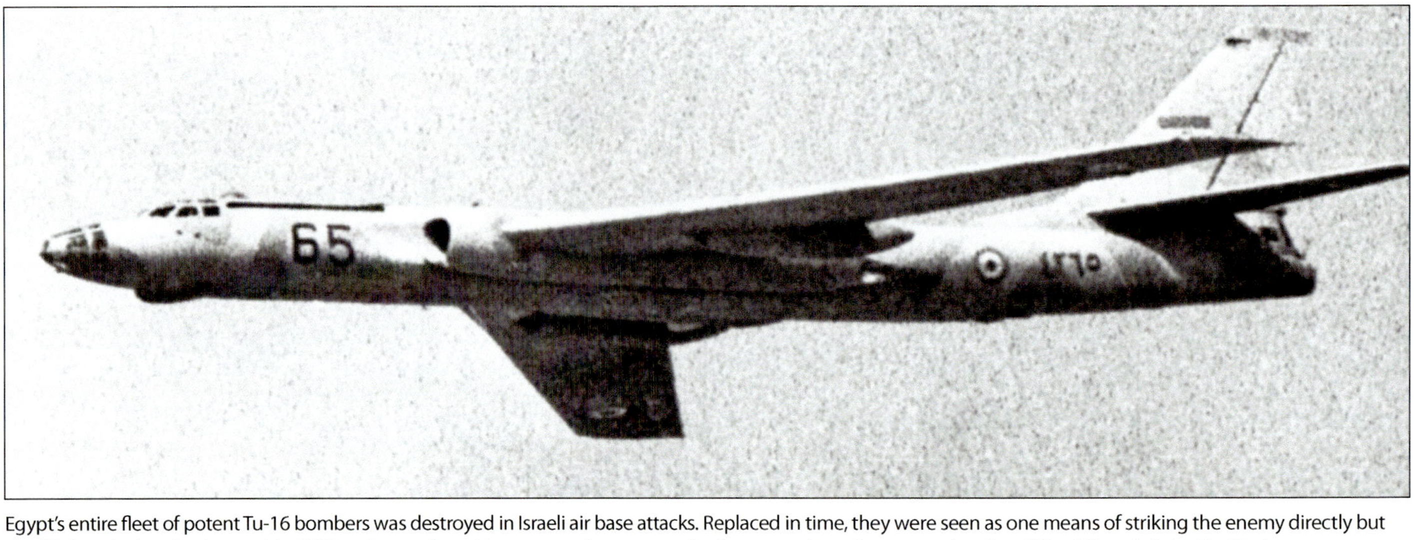

Egypt's entire fleet of potent Tu-16 bombers was destroyed in Israeli air base attacks. Replaced in time, they were seen as one means of striking the enemy directly but also likely to be lost for the trouble. UAR leaders preferred to preserve the resource for the general war they were planning. (Albert Grandolini collection)

The Soviets gained long-coveted basing rights in Egypt that helped it establish a more firm presence in the Mediterranean Sea to meet NATO strength. Among the resources brought into the country were Tu-16R naval reconnaissance aircraft finished in Egyptian colours and markings. Flown by Soviet crews, these were principally employed in monitoring the US Navy's Sixth Fleet. This Tu-16R has been intercepted by a US Navy F-4. (Albert Grandolini collection)

parsimonious with spares and delivery schedules were repeatedly ignored. It appeared to Egypt that arms were supplied in recognition of Nasser's anti-Western and anti-imperialist stance, the Soviets otherwise indifferent to Arab national aspirations. They sought to ensure continued USSR influence and basing rights in the region with no intent the weapons be used in fomenting another war frustrating other Soviet aims. This was both infuriating and humiliating to the Arabs who were unaware the problem was likely also due to limitations and inefficiencies of the Soviet economic system. Nevertheless, overall confidence was rising in the Egyptian forces as 1968 dawned and they were keen to begin expunging the indignity of their defeat.

SYRIAN RECOVERY

The Syrian Arab Republic lost an important bit of strategic territory and its armed forces experienced a severe setback during the war. The nation suffered economically and had to settle displaced citizens, but got little assistance from other Arab states. The inflexible and belligerent stance of President Nureddin al-Atassi and Deputy General Secretary, Major General Salah Jadid, plus their propensity to make trouble, tended to leave Syria on the side-lines. They were determined not to recognise nor negotiate with the Zionists. The Soviets also held these men at arm's length fearing their rabidly anti-Western and anti-Israeli rhetoric might spark another war potentially involving the superpowers. The deep abhorrence to communism by the Syrian Arab Socialist Resurrection (Baath) Party that wielded power was another detractor. Although promptly replacing most lost equipment, the USSR's generosity was more limited compared with Egypt.

When USSR President Podgorny visited Damascus in late July 1967 he cautioned Atassi that rearmament was dependent upon Syria avoiding provoking Israel. This was repeated when the Syrian President visited the USSR in August for talks on rearmament and retraining. He and War Minister and Air Force/Air Defence Commander Major General Hafez al-Assad acquiesced to unprecedented Soviet access to units for instruction and command. Advisors reached 3,000 in 1968. In return they granted the Soviet Navy port privileges at Latakia.

Immediate measures were taken to defend against any renewed hostilities. Two armoured brigades, six infantry brigades and much of the artillery had survived. This and the equipment arriving from the Soviet Union allowed creation of two mechanised brigades bringing the total to three. Defences of the approaches to Damascus, approximately 70km (45mi) from the ceasefire demarcation (Purple Line), were strengthened with three defensive lines. In September 1967 the high command produced a plan to strengthen national defences further and prepare to retake the Golan Heights. By May 1968 five of the nine brigades were suitably deployed.

Much more needed to be done. Given its weapons and terrain advantages, the performance of the army in the battles with Israel had been little short of appalling. This can largely be attributed to fractured leadership as a consequence of regime changes and 'housecleaning' of the officer corps. Syria and its armed forces had been continually weakened by an endless worry of coups (nine since the Second World War, the most recent in 1966) and clan rivalry of various ethnic and religious persuasions. There was a continuous power struggle between Atassi and General Jadid for rule, with General Assad waiting in the wings. Dissatisfied with perceived Soviet commitment, the defence leadership banned Soviet warships from the ports of Latakia and Tartus while insisting Syria increase preparation for war and more fully embrace the Palestinian cause. The Soviets were able to ameliorate these hardliners with additional arms delivered in late 1967 and early 1968. However, preparations for war remained hampered by leadership struggles and over-zealous 'lions.'

Assad replaced the army chief-of-staff with Major General Mustafa Abdul Qadir Tlass in February 1968. Tlass undertook analysis of the reasons for the defeat and consider the future structure and size of the armed forces to retake the Golan and then Palestine. Damascus spent deeply in rebuilding its armed forces. Moscow and its Bloc provided a quarter of the value in military aid. But growth was much hampered by lack of leadership cohesion, unrestricted vitriol that risked another war, police state tactics, and low morale. Although Syria was also able to acquire some munitions from the Western Europe, and China sought to lure her away from the USSR with a modest package, progress in preparing for war was slow.

The Syrian Arab Army was reorganised and expanded to five divisions (one armoured, two mechanised and two infantry) plus additional brigades and expanded special forces. The armed forces' strength rose from 120,000 to 158,000 by 1970 and the army reached 700 tanks, 900 guns and 600 armoured personnel carriers (APC). Later 50 T-54/55 tanks were added but Moscow still made deliveries in a measured manner that stretched into 1971. Combat training emphasised combined-arms principals and employed live ammunition. As with the Egyptian Army, there was to be a greater mobilisation of men with higher education standards to strengthen the officer corps. Tlass helped bring in 'good men', including those who had been purged. Consequently, 500 competent officers who had been dismissed for political unreliability were reinstated and professionalism grew.

The Syrian Arab Air Force (SyAAF) had emerged largely intact from the war given that much of the fleet had been dispersed beyond the reach of the IAF. Only a quarter of its combat jets had been destroyed. The USSR replaced these losses by the end of June 1967. The country had about 10 batteries of S-75 SAMs, but these only began to be deployed in 1968. Her requests for additional SAMs were not answered for some time. Airfields were repaired and some built new. These included hardened aircraft shelter (HAS) and underground facilities. The radar network was also restored. While Assad was nominally the SyAAF commander, deputy commander Brigadier Mohammad Assad Moukiiad held operational executive authority.

JORDANIAN REFORMATION

As with the others, the Jordanian armed forces had to regroup and replace deep equipment losses (that included 80 percent of its armour) while preparing for any additional Israeli moves against it. Army strength had fallen from 56,000 to 30,000 men in a nation of 2 million. It was resurrected largely by Major General Amer Khammash, Chief of the General Staff from October 1967 until June 1969. However, hard felt was loss of up to 40 percent of its gross domestic product and two-thirds of its arable land plus respect brought by custodianship of Jerusalem holy sites. The additional flood of Palestinians expanded the refugee camps and was a tremendous social and economic burden.[6] Palestinian residents became an even larger demographic group at approximately two-thirds of the population leaving native Jordanians at just 20 percent. The economy was deeply shaken and the usual support from Western nations had to be regained after King Hussein slandering London and Washington with claims their airmen had supported the Israelis.

King Hussein bin Talal was always seen as the 'odd man out' in the region given his moderate discourse, holding to a military of modest size with Western equipment and training, rumoured secret communications with Israel, and in 'cosying up to' Western powers. There was as much concern with threats from other Arab states and the Palestinians as from Israel. Hussein desired to provoke none while seeking assistance from several quarters.

Much work was to be done in rehabilitating the army. A Pakistani advisory mission performed a survey in 1969 and offered recommendations, then remained as trainers. Some of these reforms were enacted to include a reorganisation into a divisional structure and shallowing of command elements. The 1st Division secured the south of the country and the 2nd the north, two more division also forming. The army grew back to the 56,000 full strength. Observation posts were established along the Jordan Valley with all likely points of Israeli approach covered by artillery and aggressive patrolling. Within the border towns, armed police replaced army garrisons, but these were backed by mobile infantry platoons. Air defence was also improved together with communications security. Approximately 12,000–25,000 Iraqi troops remained stationed in the north of the country and a 1,000–6,000-man Saudi Arabian force in the south, the size of these forces fluctuating over time. Both answered to foreign leadership who were virulently anti-Israel but did not commit to anything beyond low-level harassment.

New equipment was slow in coming, from America and other Western sources, with some donated or lent by Arab states. Hussein seriously considered seeking Soviet arms that could be had more quickly and cheaply but was dissuaded by Nasser who felt a mix of arms confronting the Israelis was advisable. Military expenditure between 1967 and 1969 was equivalent to $387 million. Rebuilding the Royal Jordanian Air Force (RJAF), with just four combat aircraft having survived, was especially challenging. Given available funds its plans to adopt more modern equipment was hampered. Also, any United States of America (USA) sales to Jordan would be counterbalanced with sales to Israel for political 'optics.' Eventually the Americans and British supplied tens of millions of dollars in munitions, albeit at a slow pace. The inventory including 250 Centurion tanks, some from Egypt, and 100 M-47/M-48 Pattons as well as 230 guns.

Two of the most influential Arab leaders of the period was President Abdel Nasser of Egypt (in business suit left) and King Hussein bin Talal of Jordan (right in suit). Nasser was a near-totalitarian ruler who, immediately following the war, set his nation on a hard path to the next war. Hussein was more moderate and did not wish to suffer Israeli reprisal raids but struggled to contain the Palestinian militants in his country. (Albert Grandolini collection)

LEBANESE BACKWATER

Lebanon had always been the least active in the conflict of nations bordering Israel. The country was home to several

Palestinian refugee camps and while there was some cross-border guerrilla activity, this was comparatively minor. Lebanese participation in the Six-Day War was negligible. The tiny country was non-threatening and her armed forces were the smallest and least prepared of all the nations bordering Israel.

The all-volunteer army numbered just 11,000–14,000 personnel organised into two armoured battalions with a few dozen light tanks, 10 infantry battalions (one motorised) and one battalion of field artillery and one of air defence. Their weapons were ageing and more suited to internal security. This petite strength was partially to contain the army's potential to challenge the central government, partially owing to modest financial means, and also because the nation had no aspirations to challenge Israel or anyone else. The country had remained out of the war and this gave tremendous economic benefits, underpinned a golden age in the country through booming banking and service sectors.

Yasser Arafat (seated with sunglasses) became the face of the Palestinian resistance movement in the late 1960s. He eventually came to dominate the leadership of the PLO and el-Fatah, but struggled to unite and control the various militant factions. Arab national leaders sought to control him and the Israelis sought to kill him. (Albert Grandolini collection)

PALESTINIAN DESPONDENCY

After the war the majority of people identified as Palestinians were residing in Israel and the occupied territories. More than a million in surrounding states were living in refugee camps sponsored by the United Nations. They were largely disenfranchised and without means. Young men were inspired to seek ways of restoring their people to their homeland and to oust the Zionists. Any political settlement by Arab nations were anathema to that end. Since the Palestinians were a stateless people with no military, this suggested an insurgency and guerrilla warfare.

The surrounding confrontation states, with wealthy 'oil states' aiding in funding, used the eagerness of these fighters for their own ends in harassing Israel. Particularly the conservative oil-rich countries preferred to keep the Palestinians at arm's length given their strong streak of radicalism. The irregular warfare did not jeopardise national forces but supported the aspiration of return of the Palestinians. This, it was hoped, would drain IDF resources from the fronts and money from Israel's coffers while undermining her image among potential international supporters. For a time immediately following the war this struggle was the most active and visible aspect of the conflict and attracted admiration across the Arab world plus additional Palestinian recruits. Lacking the means to effectively engage the IDF, actions were usually civilian killings and national infrastructure sabotage.[7] Such had been a constant presence since before Israel's independence with hundreds of attacks. She responded as before with cross-border raids and clandestine operations within the Arab countries – and now the occupied territories – to suppress these forces and eliminate leadership.

The principal political representation of the Palestinians was the Palestine Liberation Organization (PLO). The Palestinian National Covenant endorsed the armed struggle with Israel in the context of a popular revolution to liberate Palestinian land, ejecting almost all the Jews, and establishment of a state. The PLO was intended to serve as an umbrella organisation for numerous liberation bodies to undertake the armed struggle. The organisation was ultimately unable to coral the diverse militant groups for coordinated efforts, especially given controls and limitations imposed by the various host countries. Most of these states had Palestinian units in its ranks at various times. National leaders always ensured that these armed foreigners did not become powerful enough to challenge them. Consequently, their effectiveness remained short of desired.

The Palestine National Liberation Movement, or el-Fatah, was the principal instigator of the irregular warfare. Dominated by Yasser Arafat, it took its inspiration from various world revolutionary movements. Consequently, many of the Palestinian militant organisations had socialist and Marxist leanings, seeking a peoples' uprising against the oppressor – adopting some of the lingo of activist movements throughout the world. Fatah had been run principally by Syrian Intelligence. An Egyptian counterpart was the Palestine Liberation Army (PLA) with a brigade in Egypt-proper, another in Syria, and one in Iraq. There the PLA trained and were directed by those nations' armies.

The Palestinian movement was as hard hit by the June 1967 defeat as the Arab nation states. The PLO's leader, Ahmed Shukairy, fled Jerusalem first to Amman and then Damascus while the organisation split into factions. An ever-turning anarchic kaleidoscope of up to a dozen organisations claimed to represent the Palestinians and each had their own fighters, collectively referred to as fedayeen (those who sacrifice). Further friction was caused by the fact many of these organisations were aligned with national sponsors who sought to exploit them for their own interests that sometimes worked at cross-purposes with other nations. Disenchanted with the dysfunction, the Arab League cancelled it $41 million subsidy to the PLO.[8]

Only an alliance of Arab armies launching an overwhelming, coordinated attack to defeat the IDF and occupy Israel had any hope of destroying the 'Zionist Entity' and permit establishment of a Palestinian state – provided the invaders did not simply carve up and subsume the land as they had in 1949. Yet, even under Nasser's leadership the national goals of individual countries never aligned to permit this. May 1967 represented the closest he had come to achieving the coalition, but Israel's victory greatly dampened any eagerness for a rematch on that scale. Consequently, the Six-Day War drove Palestinians' dream of return farther away. The Arabs had to be content with tormenting Israel and causing gratuitous bloodshed to gain some measure of satisfaction without attracting too great an IDF reaction. The sacrifice of Palestinian fighters would continue contributing to this end. Arafat was quoted as saying, 'Palestine is the cement that holds the Arab world together, or it is the explosive that blows it apart.'

ISRAEL ADJUSTS

The IDF had emerged from the war very much intact, with tremendous experience and confidence. She had suffered 338 dead, 1,450 wounded, 11 missing and 61 tanks destroyed out of a total 122 tanks knocked out (the difference being those repaired). Filled with their success and praise from military experts worldwide, they perhaps did not analyse the war as carefully as they should have nor appreciate how much the errors of their adversaries had contributed to the victory.

Israel's was an atypical military, always struggling for funds and suitable equipment. A small country, Israel was manpower-constrained and so it relied on a proportionately small professional force to hold the enemy until reserves could be called up. Full mobilisation required 72 hours and drew 20 percent of the nation's workforce such that it could not economically be sustained for long. The air force was to keep the skies clear to ensure the mobilisation occurred with no interference. With little or no strategic depth, Israel relied on intelligence services to provide sufficient warning of attack such that the fight could be brought to the enemy first in a pre-emptive action. This would be executed with fast armoured strikes aided by airpower.

The active force consisted of approximately 50,000 conscripts backed by around 11,500 professionals and approximately 18,000 reservists in uniform at any given time. Reservists performed routine service periods (typically a month per year) until age 49 for men and 34 for women. Of a population of approximately 2.8 million, mobilisation brought the force to about 275,000 of whom 30 percent were women in non-combat roles. The compulsory service in the regular army was 30 months for men and 18 months for women. Officers were comparatively youthful with generals usually in their 40s.

This 'citizen army' was noted for its egalitarianism that was characterised by lax adherence to protocols and informality that extended to individual roles and responsibilities. As the state was still young, without deep tradition or extensive regulations, much was done on improvisation and this extended to the military as well. The IDF was known for a shallow chain of command in a small country that permitted rapid reaction to exigencies in combat and unit commanders given freedom to adjust tactics as required. Historically only cabinet members regularly discussed defence policy, with the prime minister frequently also holding the defence portfolio. The legislature seldom engaged on such matters and the defence budget was commonly passed with little debate.

Although Israel had suffered far fewer loses in the war than its adversaries, the continuing conflict and rearming of Arab militaries made it imperative that the IDF replace lost equipment plus progressively upgrade systems to meet expanding threats. Much of its equipment was aged, with upgrades reaching their limits. Acquisition had always been paced by willing sellers, sufficient budget, and debate over priorities. The air force was then getting 50 percent of defence outlays, the armoured corps 30 percent, and other arms the remainder. There was never enough money to equip to fully modern standards and the budget was stretched so thin that training was constrained to avoid the operational expense. Unlike those nations supplied immediately by the Soviet Union, Israel had to pay for weapons with hard currency. The long-standing French supply was rapidly drying up with the embargo on arms deliveries to the region imposed by President Charles de Gaulle prior to the war. This almost exclusively affected Israel and was maintained after because of Israel's conduct during the war and de Gaulle's pique at having his admonition not to initiate hostilities ignored. France sought to increase her influence on the 'Arab Street' and this meant turning away from Israel.

The Americans had begun to sell Israel weaponry and this progressively increased in volume in meeting increasing Soviet penetration of the oil-rich region. These Cold War fears were by no means played down by the Israelis. The USA sought to 'balance' arms being provided to Arab states but at first sold only 'defensive' equipment. However, as sales expanded almost exponentially in step with Soviet support for Israel's adversaries and mounting combat, such constraints fell away.

The Israelis had been manufacturing some military consumables and equipment spares. It also performed major rework of vehicles and aircraft. This was always challenging given that the country was

Israel was ecstatic at the outcome of the war, threats receding with defeat of the Arab armies confronting her and captured territory as buffer. Revelling in the praise from around the world, she celebrated in many ways. Among these was a display of captured enemy hardware in Tel Aviv. (Albert Grandolini collection)

The A-4Hs provided a significant range and air-to-ground weapons delivery capacity. Three of the first such machines carry the 109 Squadron badge in this image. The aerial refuelling capability and arresting hook for emergency recovery were new features to the IAF. (BIAF – Israel Aerospace Magazine)

like an island, with everything not derived directly from the land coming in by sea or air. It was soon producing 80 percent of the IDF's ammunition requirements and 90 percent of its light and medium arms. Three percent of the nation's budget was devoted to military research and development. As the defence budget increased much of the money was spent inside the country as the arms industry likewise grew and employed more of the workforce. Soon a quarter of industrial output was devoted to defence. There was a tendency to favour local production even if this meant higher cost and a delay in acquiring needed armaments. These costly efforts were partially offset by selling such products and services internationally. Owing to frequent operational use of the equipment and Israeli reputation for combat success, it became a selling point that the products were employed by the IDF.

The new geo-military situation meant defending longer borders, building IDF infrastructure in the captured territories, attempting to match enemy armaments, and dealing with continuing armed conflict. The size of Israel's standing armed forces grew over 40 percent in the years after the war. Fortunately, the glowing reputation of the IDF helped attract high-quality conscripts to combat arms and willingness to serve beyond the minimum obligation. This was also assisted by increased awarding of medals and other forms of recognition not previously common. The spartan nature of the force began to fade, staffs grew, and more money was turned to creature comforts. The brigadier rank was introduced and so all above stepped up in rank; the chief-

Israel had to wait a few more months than the Arabs in receiving replacement aircraft following the June 1967 war. Two squadrons of A-4Hs were taken up beginning in December 1967 to inaugurate what would become a tremendous American reequipping of the Israel Defence Forces over the next few years of conflict and decades beyond. The first machine is offloaded from a freighter in Haifa harbour on 26 December still wrapped in its protective sealant. (BIAF – Israel Aerospace Magazine)

Most of the conflict nations were manufacturing at least ammunition while Israel (shown) took this a step further and were producing weapons, mostly under license. Local production supported the economy and built industrial capacity. The IDF got most of its light arms and nearly all its ammunition locally, to include bombs, rockets and missiles. (Israel GPO)

of-staff became a Lieutenant General instead of a Major General. The enlarged military seemed to be present everywhere in the country, was held in high regard, and was full of confidence. All almost uniformly denigrated Arab military capabilities.

The army moved from brigades brought together in ad hoc formations for operations to fixed divisional organisations. Amour continued to reign supreme, especially given their contributions during the war. The number of tanks and brigades more than doubling. New Patton tanks from the USA and Centurions improved in Israeli shops, plus captured T-54/55 tanks, helped modernised the corps. Infantry, mechanised and otherwise, got the short end of the stick in terms of new vehicles and weapons plus lagging behind the tanks during offensives. Artillery was even further marginalised and underfunded.

Table 1: Arms Purchases and Deliveries, 1967–1973 ($ million)[9]

Metric	Country	1967	1968	1969	1970	1971	1972	1973
Sales	Egypt	216	109	88	662	415	181	542
	Syria	110	80	22	71	135	311	529
	Jordan	52	94	22	40	59	82	80
	Lebanon	2	negligible	16	3	11	24	16
	Israel	99	539	156	146	429	554	218*
Deliveries	Egypt	176	130	112	685	373	283	480
	Syria	50	43	39	62	110	150	720
	Jordan	34	40	58	74	41	40	56
	Lebanon	-	34	21	3	2	24	18
	Israel	100	133	131	324	413	322	279

* Excludes the $1 billion of sales by the USA in July–December 1973 because the American data were for fiscal years and sales associated with the October 1973 war would skew the comparison.

Table 2: Heavy Weapons Transfers, 1967–1973[10]

Category	Country	Number	Weapons
Armoured Fighting Vehicles	Egypt	≈800 ≈550 ≈200 ? PD 90	T-54 tank T-55 tank PT-76 light tank BMP-1 IFV T-62 tank
	Syria	<100 ≈300 ≈375 <500 ≈80 ≈200	T-34-85 T-54 tank T-55 tank T-62 tank PT-76 light tank BRDM-2 with Malyutka missiles
	Jordan	(200) PD 52 40	Centurion tanks M-48 tanks Ferret armoured cars
	Lebanon	22 (74) PD	AMX-13/105 light tank AML-60/90 armoured car
	Israel	≈522 (200) PD ≈150 ≈50	Centurion tanks M-48A1 tanks M-60A1 tanks AML-60/90 armoured cars
	Egypt	(100) (300) CD (200) CD ≈50 (50) CD ≈100 ≈12	T-12 100mm/2A19 TG D-20 152mm TG D-30 122mm TG S-23 180mm TG M-160 160mm mortar BM-21 122mm MLRS Luna rocket
Artillery Systems	Syria	<300 ≈300 (300) CD (300) CD (200) CD <25 CD x100s CD ≈200 ≈100 ≈300 ≈12	BS-3 100mm TG D-30 122mm TG M-30 122mm TG A-19 122mm TG ML-20 152mm TG M-160 160mm mortar PM-43 120mm mortar BM-14 140mm MLRS BM-21 Grad 122mm MLRS BM-24 240mm MLRS Luna rocket
	Jordan	≈30 ≈35 ≈126	M-101A1 105mm TG M-52A1 105mm SPG M-109 155mm SPG
	Lebanon	20 or 24 ≈15	M-30 122mm TG MO-120-M65 120mm mortar
	Israel	≈60 ≈90 (100) CD (50) CD 60 ? PD ≈125 ≈40	M-114 155mm TG M-101A1 203mm TG M-73 120mm mortar M-58 160mm mortar M-109 155mm SPG M-109A1B 155mm SPG M-107 175mm SPG M-110 203mm SPG

Definitions: CD=continued delivery (started pre-war), IFV=infantry fighting vehicle, MLRS=Multiple Rocket Launch System (self-propelled), PD=partial delivery (continued beyond October 1973), SPG=self-propelled gun/howitzer, TG=towed gun/howitzer

2

PHOENIX FROM THE ASHES

Rehabilitation of the Egyptian armed forces was to be an extended and complex affair with organisational and cultural changes. Pulling from the front was President Nasser who wished to resume hostilities with Israel at the earliest opportunity with an eventual goal of liberation Sinai and the Gaza Strip. Pulling from behind was the Soviet Union who did not relish another war that risked another defeat of Russian arms. The replacement of weapons alone could not ensure a resurgence of Arab arms. The Egyptian armed forces' prestige collapsed when it became apparent the June 1967 debacle was due to the leadership of incompetent officers. Some 'housecleaning' was in order.

PRUNING THE TREE

Gamal Abdel Nasser had an almost messianic allure within the Arab world. By deposing a corrupt monarchy, ejecting Western influence via firm stand and war, gaining assistance from the USSR, instituting agrarian reforms, and restructuring the economy along socialist lines, he gained vast popular appeal well beyond Egypt. However, in the early 1960s this had diminished with inability to unite Arab nations, devolution to a one-party system with virtual autocratic authority, failed weapons development programmes, the military stymied in the Yemen civil war, and an economic downturn. The Six-Day War only amplified the problems and exposed the armed forces as disastrously deficient. Under pressure from his Minister of War, Shems al-Din Badran, his Vice President, Deputy Supreme Commander and Commander-in-Chief Field Marshal Mohamed Abdel Hakim Amer (Nasser was Supreme Commander), and most of his other senior generals, Nasser announced his resignation on 9 June. There were emotional protests in the streets by hundreds of thousands appealing for him to stay on, along with an entreaty from the National Assembly and the chosen successor refusing to serve. Nasser reversed his decision on the 10th. With this 'mandate', Nasser set out to renew self-confidence with four objectives; rebuilding national military strength, seeking a diplomatic solution, unifying the Arabs behind Egypt, and holding together the home front.

Much of the general staff resigned or were sacked. Badran and Amer resigned on the 11th as well as Chief-of-Staff Lieutenant General Mohamed Fawzi. Nasser had to ensure competent officers who would not plot *coups d'état* against him – the standard means of regime change in the region. General Fawzi became commander-in-chief of the armed forces on 11 June. Amin Howeidi, a retired army officer who had long held diplomatic and ministerial appointments, became War Minister and head of Military Intelligence. He relinquished the former post to Fawzi in March 1968. Lieutenant General Abdul Munim Riadh, formerly commanding air defences and leading the Jordanian front during the war, became chief-of-staff on the 11th. A month later Lieutenant General Ahmed Ismail Ali became Director of Operations. There followed a reorganisation of the command structure.

Nasser's old friend Amer initially ignored discharge from all his roles and blamed the defeat on the president for refusing to attack first. The field marshal had been very popular within the army thanks to his generosity to friends and supporters, assigning civilian jobs and perks while in uniform. On 11 June some 600 officers, including more than 50 senior commanders with four lieutenant generals commanding thousands of soldiers, briefly besieged army headquarters in remonstration. The possibility of a coup by pro-Amer officers was very real especially as 200 loyal officers and kinsmen from his home village of Minya provided a bodyguard protecting his villa at Giza where he holed up. Four armoured vehicles drove towards Nasser's home, the Presidential Guard being on the Suez front. Nasser dissembled, promising a committee to deal with the rebels' grievances, but slept with a pistol under his pillow.

The president ordered a delegation consisting of new Minister of War Howeidi, Interior Minister Shaarawi Gomaand Jumma, the Director of General Intelligence (and Nasser's 'fixer') Sami Sharaf to neutralise Amer. For this Nasser invited Amer to dinner in his home on 25 August and, when he arrived, troops loyal to Nasser surrounded the house ready to arrest the field marshal. Amer was met by Vice Presidents Zakkria Mohieddin and Hussein el-Shafei as well as the Speaker of the National Assembly Anwar Sadat. Nasser departed and Amer then went into the bathroom. Emerging with a glass of water, he told everyone to inform the president that he had taken poison. Nasser, who had changed for bed, did not believe it and said, 'If he was going to do that he would have done so after what happened in Sinai.' In fact, Amer went home to find his friends burning documents in the garden and they surrendered at 0400. Three truck-loads of weapons were removed from the building while Amer was firmly restricted to his home.

President Abdel Nasser and Field Marshall Hakim Amer in happier times, signing an arms sale deal with Czechoslovakia. The two had long been friends, had conspired together to overthrow the old monarchy, and worked to establish a new socialist Egypt. However, Amer would accumulate ever-more authority over the military and even into civil affairs while mismanaging the armed forces. The army's poor performance in the Six-Day War can be laid largely at his feet, although Nasser's acquiescence to Amer's dysfunction contributed. (Albert Grandolini collection)

On 4 September Amer, Badran and other military and security leaders were charged with plotting a coup to reinstate Amer and trying to end an inquiry into responsibility for the defeat. A total of 149 people were arrested and questioned, including former Interior Minister Abbas Radwan, former Chief of Intelligence General Salah Nasser, former division commander General Osman Nasser and former head of the commando school Lieutenant Colonel Galal Haridi. A special court chaired by Vice President el-Shafei tried them beginning in January 1968. After three months the five senior officers were jailed for life with hard labour, two got 15 years hard labour, 30 were jailed and 14 acquitted. On 11 September General Riadh called on Amer, informed him he was being moved, and had him escorted to detention in another house. Three days later Amer contacted his family seeking books and medicine but the next day his family were informed he had been buried at Minya after having committed suicide, although the family have always claimed he was poisoned.[1]

Amer's death, without an embarrassing trial, removed a potentially divisive influence. Nasser warned the public that there were counter-revolutionaries and Israeli agents seeking to take advantage of the circumstances. Under this cover, Nasser quashed dissent within the armed forces in late August and early September. As many as 500–800 officers were purged.[2] Trials were held, mostly in secret, and many were convicted of misconduct and even treason. For example, air force senior staff were relieved and tried. The chief and the Director of Air Defence, were sentenced to life imprisonment while others were acquitted. There were public protests over what appeared lenient sentences. Retrials meted out more severe punishments. Hence, Nasser escaped culpability for his own failures. All this leadership instability deepened the disquiet in the ranks and negatively impacted recovery.

The task of the shuffled leadership was to whip the Egyptian Army into shape. Immediately after the war Nasser called in the general staff and gave them a dressing down, calling them 'cowards and bastards', again working to divert blame from himself for the nation's ills. Regardless, he needed the staff to confront the Israelis, with Generals Fawzi and Riadh (the rank of field marshal being eliminated) the most responsible. Nasser's friend and confidant Mohamed Hassanein Heikal, editor of the newspaper *Al-Ahram*, described Fawzi as 'a cruel disciplinarian', a view apparently shared by the president, and noted 'he rode roughshod over all human considerations.' However, his associated General Mohamed Gamasy observed his cruelty was a much-needed quality at a time when military discipline had significantly declined. Heikal described Riadh was a technocrat 'obsessed by the need to fight' and believing a peaceful solution with the Israelis was impossible. Gamasy also noted that Riadh possessed both the experience and broad strategic vision needed to produce pragmatic policies. He and Fawzi complemented each other.[3]

Protests of disorder in the country continued into the new year. Nasser closed the universities temporarily and imposed press censorship. He reorganised the party and shuffled the government. Supreme Commander and President, he also took the premiership, eliminated vice presidents and the deputy supreme commander, and also assumed the post of Secretary General of the party. His cabinet had more civilians and fewer military members but Nasser held almost sole authority. He continued to paint Israel as an existential threat to focus the anger of the nation away from his poor management and increasing dictatorial behaviour. Yet, he remained depressed and seemed a shadow of his former self.

UP AND RUNNING

Fawzi and General Ismail Ali, the latter as Suez front commander, had rallied forces for a defence along the waterway using whatever equipment could be found. Of the 21 active and reserve brigades deployed to Sinai in May 1967 only three from the 4th Armoured Division re-crossed the waterway and even they were badly tattered. There were just two infantry brigades, one a reservist unit, and two artillery brigades that had remained west of the canal. So desperate was the situation that the brigade-sized Presidential Guard was rushed to the front. Within a month the Egyptians had five infantry and two armoured brigades as well as five commando battalions deployed on the canal with the other brigades in reserve. Three infantry brigades were already crossing the Red Sea from Yemen.

Appearances can be deceiving. This image shows a formation of UAR combat troops in front and common worker-soldiers in back. Much work was done post-war to improve the combat readiness of the former and the education of the latter to handle increasingly sophisticated equipment. (Albert Grandolini collection)

After a surge, Nasser wound down his forces' costly involvement in the civil war that had engaged 40,000 troops. The remaining six brigades, including one armoured and one artillery, followed by 16 October 1967. Soviet arms shipments meant two armoured brigades were reformed or reequipped by the end of the year. Added to these forces were a 4,000-man PLA Brigade, an Algerian brigade, and the Kuwaiti 6th Yarmuk Battalion which had arrived in Egypt during June.

Nasser gave Marshal Zakharov and Colonel General Lashchenko carte blanche to use these forces and any other resources to build up the defences on the front. Within a month there was a 'trip wire' capability and by November, equipped with new weapons, the forces were firm enough to meet any Israeli crossing attempt. The defences were formed per Soviet doctrine with three lines of trenches and bunkers in an essentially continuous line of troop-presence. Apart from a brief scare in late 1967 generated by IDF troop movements, there was never an imminent threat of a large-scale Israeli crossing of the canal.

All bridges across the waterway had been demolished by Egyptian engineers and the waterway posed a formidable obstacle. At up to 24m (79ft) deep it was described by military tacticians as 'the world's biggest anti-tank ditch.' Neither opponent possessed sufficient bridging nor ferrying equipment to storm the far bank. Neither had trained for such an operation. Consequently, the Israelis could defend Sinai with light forces while Egypt could rebuild her strength with a fair degree of security.

Nasser empowered Generals Fawzi and Riadh with rehabilitating the army and preparing for war with Israel to liberate lost territory, convinced that force was the only message the Zionists understood. With much to do, they set out with determination, foresight, and skill. In January 1968 Fawzi chaired a meeting to produce a strategic framework for achieving the objective, but it was clear a long period of preparation and training lay ahead. The president set a goal of being prepared for the invasion within three years, although he accepted that this may require up to eight years. It was decided to test proficiency in the new weapons and to probe the defences by conducting a gradual escalation of force along the canal in three phases; Stabilisation or Steadfastness (*summud*), Confrontation (*muwajahah*), then Challenge and Response (*tahadee wa radeah*).[4] The nation could then move to liberation of Sinai to Victory (*nasr*).

The national strategy was announced in two broadcasts, making clear Nasser's determination to lead the nation to another war with Israel. On 23 November 1967 he said, 'We shall choose the opportune moment. First and foremost, we need time to complete our military preparations so that when a time of operation comes, we shall not be on the defensive … we shall attack to cleanse our land which the enemy is occupying.'[5] In another speech, printed in *Al-Ahram* on 21 January 1968, he added, 'The first priority, the absolute priority, in this battle is the military front, for we must realise that the enemy will not withdraw unless we force him to withdraw through fighting. Indeed, there can be no hope of any political solution unless the enemy realises that we are capable of forcing him to withdraw through fighting.'[6] In a speech on 10 March 1968 Nasser laid before his troops his vision of the path to final victory beginning with firm stand (*summud*) then preventative defence (*dafaa waqaai*), deterrence (*al-rade*) and liberation (*tahrir*) phases. A few weeks later he informed the armed forces senior leaders another military round with Israel was inevitable and they must liquidate completely the consequences of the June 1967 war, but warned that the battle will be long and bitter.

Field Marshall Amer had built a cult of personality around himself along with a large number of devoted officers. He was permitted to assume almost total and unquestioned authority over the armed forces, side-lining the general staff. He marginalised Nasser's authority and largely ignored civilian authority. The benefit of other viewpoints and leadership expertise was weakened. The army expended considerable resources on internal security, working against threats to the revolution. Training had atrophied or was hollow. Promotions were largely based on patronage, favouritism, and cliques rather than performance. Reports reflected what senior officers wanted to hear rather than true effectiveness or capabilities. Operational proficiency was lacking. Focus was on defensive tactics rather than offense.

Nasser's ambition of retaking occupied lands required significant growth and reorganisation of the armed forces plus additional arms, facilities, and extensive retraining. The resources of the nation would be mobilised and directed to the task of preparing for war. While working to these ends while undoing Amer's dysfunction and instilling inter-service cooperation, Nasser and Fawzi still made almost all the high-level decisions themselves and so continued to undermine the general staff. Nasser retained almost complete authority, able to dismiss personnel and even order executions without due process.

There was an investigation and assessment of the failings leading to the defeat. A contingent of 91 senior Soviet officers conducted their own evaluation and suggest paths forward. Their conclusions were that the army needed major reform and retraining. The USSR was ready to help implement changes and provide instruction. However, the Soviet Union had had no direct combat experience since the Second World War save for minor contributions in regional conflicts, and reports of their equipment's effectiveness came mostly second-hand. The Egyptians would come to judge Soviet instruction and tactics as outdated and unsuitable for their circumstances as demonstrated by repeated combat failings.

The number of Soviet advisors reached 3,000–4,000 by January 1970. Their role in reconstructing and improving the armed forces was slow and frustrating. The language barrier and cultural differences was an unending problem especially given a dearth of interpreters. The advisors' disdain for the competence and dedication to hard work of their Arab counterparts was sometimes little concealed. The divergent opinions about whether Soviet equipment and doctrine had been proven deficient in the war also created tensions. Given the advisors' crucial role, Nasser had to order officers to obey them, even if of lower grade. Offering advice on formulation of strategy and tactics, they were initially active at the battalion level but were soon attached to units down to brigades. However, their influence was felt at all levels of command and field organisations. The advisors also had a hand in planning operations. The Soviets usually advised restraint with respect to challenging the IDF, and their cautious attitudes angered the Egyptians. While the USSR wanted the Arabs to engage Israel and undo the war's outcome, they also did not want them to fail in the attempt.

The army's focus was shifted from internal security to another war with Israel – although fear of coups and counter-revolutionaries, with attention to political 'currents', was never far from the minds of senior personnel. The armed forces began to be reformed along Soviet lines and sought to expand nearly four-fold by late 1970. The command structure was reoriented and simplified, and forces were joined into armies or corps. Housing these forces in the eastern desert and opposite the canal, while enabling movement and resupply, required a considerable construction effort for roads, water pipelines and storage facilities, power distribution, and the like. The de-facto 1st Army held the Cairo District. The 2nd Field Army was formed in November 1968 to control all the forces in the canal area and commanded by deputy army commander Major General Adli Said. However, as the canal front extended along the Rea Sea coast to Adabiya Port (170km/106mi) and an average 60km (37mi) deep, it was too large for effective command and control solely by 2nd Army. Under Russian pressure, summer 1968 saw preparations for activation of the 3rd Army which would take over the southern half of the front from Great Bitter Lake. However, due to problems assembling a qualified staff, its formation was delayed until November when it was activated under Major General Qadri Uthman, succeeded early in 1969 by Major General Mohammed Fahaiq Bourini.

The armed forces was only slowly rebuilt and had a long road to parity with the IDF. Its offensive options were greatly limited through summer 1970. By the end of 1967 it had about a dozen brigades, four armoured or mechanised. By February 1968 the army had reached 70 percent of its pre-war strength but still faced a shortfall of 13,000 vehicles. It expanded to 22 brigades by the end of 1968, including six armoured/mechanised and one parachute, organised into four or five divisions. Two more divisions were being formed and the Russians had agreed to equip them fully. Divisional-size exercises were undertaken for the first time. Tank battalions were reequipped with modern Soviet main battle tanks, replacing Second World War vintage equipment. Battlefield mobility was enhanced with modern APCs. Manning remained an acute problem. While the forces were in good condition, they were still not prepared to go onto the offensive against the IDF's air and armoured superiority. The Soviet advisors watched progress with exasperation as numerous deficiencies in planning and preparation remained apparent.

Nasser continued some foreign adventures, though on a smaller scale than Yemen. A small contingent of Egyptian troops, including UARAF elements, were active in the Biafra war in Nigeria from 1968 through 1970. They did likewise in Sudan during 1969–1973. These efforts helped build experience.

Restoring the UARAF and making ready for a rematch with Israeli's triumphant air force required many more aircraft, pilots, and air bases. Personnel numbers and qualities were particular focuses. The dozens of junior officers disciplined and replaced during the purges, mostly for political reasons and questionable allegiance to Nasser, was to the detriment of morale. Before the war the shortages of everyone from mechanics to pilots was so acute that many new aircraft were simply stored in their crates. The number of aircraft eventually grew beyond pre-war level and more were sought. Most of the remaining airbases had a single runway, no technical units with runway repair specialty, plus inadequate hangar and HAS space able to withstand air attack. New airfields and added runways, plus hundreds of HAS began to be constructed. The new air force chief, Air Vice Marshal Madkour Ahmed Abu al-Ezz, was named on 11 June 1967 but relieved on 23 October for challenging Fawzi in front of Nasser.[7] His replacement was Air Vice Marshal Mustafa Shalaby el-Hinnawi.

Finding suitable personnel to operate increasingly sophisticated armaments was a challenge. Of 350,000 men becoming available for conscription every year only 120,000 were assessed as fit and only tens of thousands were actually inducted. The majority of the populace were uneducated Fellaheen and urban poor eking out a living as labourers. Only 30 percent of enlisted personnel possessed even an elementary school education.[8] Consequently, reform included educating soldiers while more college graduates were recruited

This IAF reconnaissance image shows a hardened aircraft shelter under construction at a UARAF air base. Egypt undertook a massive military construction effort after the June 1967 defeat that included new airfields, improving existing bases, and a greatly expanded air defence system. They were determined that the Israelis would not be able to repeat their surprise air attack. (Albert Grandolini collection)

or drafted. Some induction standards were relaxed and women volunteers were also accepted for clerical duties in rear areas – an unusual step in the largely Muslim country. The number of citizens with the aptitude for roles such as combat pilot was estimated at one per one million citizens in a country of 33–35 million inhabitants.[9] To gain the most benefit from training investment, the draftees, previously obligated to serve for three years, were now required to remain in the service until the captured territory was liberated – or indefinitely. Families were told to simply forget their sons. Effectively, Egypt was mobilising its people amongst other national resources for the continuing struggle with Israel.

Ironically a significant heritage of the Amer-era was his expansion of the military education system. The Military Academy, responsible for the training of both army and air force officers, expanded its curriculum to introduce more specialised topics and sought to improve overall quality. The Military Technical Academy, established

Above: An Egyptian air force HAS seen from ground level shows the blast doors and other features. Services worldwide adopted these structures to protect aircraft during airbase attack following the Israeli success in the Six-Day War, and also the Indo-Pakistan war of 1965, in destroying enemy aircraft on the ground. (M. P. H.)

Right: The catastrophic outcome of the war brought new men to key positions in Egypt's military. Lieutenant General Fawzi (middle) became commander-in-chief of the armed forces and also War Minister. The new air force commander was Air Vice Marshal Abu al-Ezz but served little more than four months before being relieved by Air Vice Marshal Shalaby el-Hinnawi (left). One of his senior deputies was Colonel Hosni Mubarak (right), later chief-of-staff of the UARAF. They are seen here visiting the Egyptian air academy. (M. C. S. Eman)

by Amer in 1958 to provide officer engineers and technicians, revised its curriculum and from November 1968 developed five specialised courses. University graduates, who were previously exempt, were now recruited and conscripted, raising the overall officer quality. Still, there was a shortage of officers given those killed or discharged and imprisoned.

Egypt especially lacked experienced men and those with a technical background. However, there were still senior officers who had fallen afoul of Amer and been side-lined into the training organisations but who would command new brigades and divisions. The military education institutions could produce only 3,000 junior officers a year. It was decided to make up the numbers by conscripting previously exempt university graduates or to use conscripts who had graduated from secondary schools. These were sent on four-to-five-month training courses which led to their commissioning as War Service officers to command units at platoon or company level. Some 30,000 such men ultimately passed through training schools by October 1973. This officer shortage partially explains why the army's combat forces remained at 180,000 men until 1970 and why Nasser welcomed Soviet advisors.

The officers were essentially a privileged class with many recruited by patronage, favours, the connections of powerful families, and political reliability rather than professional capability. They were by-and-large more focussed on the societal benefits of service than a military career with commitment to national duty, and were not devoted to hard work. It was a corps rife with favouritism, nepotism, devotion to specific senior officers, and fear of purges. The upper ranks spent a good deal of energy on political intrigue, usually seeking personal gain. Promotions and decorations were a means of ensuring loyalty to individual officers or to lift morale rather than recognising sterling performance. Following the purges of 1967–1968 – over a thousand officers in total – many who remained possessed outdated experience or were poor leaders.

Officers were commonly university educated, from middle or upper classes. They typically led from the rear and performed all the thinking while the lower ranks performed rote tasks. There was a significant cultural, educational, and physical separation between the officers and the common soldier with too few NCOs bridging the gap. The time officers spent away from their units was unacceptably high.

The army needed a substantial culture change that did not come quickly or easily. It was to defend the nation and not just the political order. The new professional soldiers would be promoted based upon merit. Allegiance to the state, devotion to unit and mission, and hard work were all to be emphasised. However, doctrine and tactics were largely rigid. Personal initiative and criticism were still discouraged. Additionally, each service acted largely on its own with little in the way of coordination and combined-arms doctrine.

Before June 1967 it had been forbidden to discuss enemy capabilities and make comparisons. Pilots captured by the enemy were prohibited from returning to flying. Correcting these errors, the enemy was now studied in detail, especially as they were reengaged over the coming years. Tactics and behaviour assessed to be beneficial were adopted. Nasser now sought a pragmatic assessment of the enemy and, at Heikal's suggestion, the Presidential Office's Centre of Palestinian and Zionism Studies (later renamed the Centre for Political and Strategic Studies) was established under General Taha al-Magdub for a more professional political-military study of Israel.

The rehabilitation proceeded slower than hoped given demonstrated performance of the combat forces, degradation through combat, and long periods between Soviet agreement to supply arms and actual delivery – some clearly intended to restrain their clients.

The army did begin equipping and training for a cross-canal operation. It had begun acquiring amphibious tanks, landing craft, and mobile bridging equipment – some designed and manufactured in-country – and began training for the cross-canal operation. The first such exercise was in fall 1968.[10] Training was initially conducted near the Suez, on the parallel Sweetwater Canal, but this attracted IDF 'attention.' Another location northwest of Cairo, Wadi El Natrun (also identified as the El Faiyum depression and Lake Qarun), saw ever-growing use as training intensified. Other areas and the western desert became sites for training in combined-arms exercises unlike anything the Egyptian Army had ever undertaken. All this was monitored by Israeli reconnaissance flights.

3

SETTLING IN

The June 1967 ceasefire left a victorious army looking across the line at humiliated and angry opposition armies eager to prove their mettle and undo the enemy gains. With the potential for a final settlement of the conflict appearing bleak, these forces settled in for a potentially long confrontation. In the case of Israel this included establishing a military occupation of captured lands and people while building defensive positions. Diplomatic positions also hardened and presaged a period of stalemate.

THE OCCUPATION

Israel's success in the Six-Day War brought her immense joy and satisfaction, but also many new challenges. She became occupier of vast stretches of territory (officially Administered Territories).[1] The Sinai and Gaza Strip offered previously unavailable strategic depth. Likewise, the Golan Heights served as a buffer to past harassment by Syria. The borders were more defensible, but the extended logistical lines of communications burdened by lack of a railroad network could present problems in another general war. The West Bank was also viewed as Judea and Samaria, historical elements of ancient Israel. The 'liberation' of the whole of Jerusalem, with its holy sites, held particular emotional rewards. With the seat of Israeli government in the western quarter, Jerusalem was unified and the remainder effectively annexed by the end of June 1967.[2] Holding these lands and preparing to meet any aggression required considerable military presence with extended lines of communication and infrastructure improvement, all demanding a substantial financial outlay. These also came with approximately 1.1 million Arab inhabitants. The occupation became a troubling military, civil, monetary, and legal issue.

There was a period of clean-up following the war. Israel sorted through the detritus to glean insight into enemy equipment,

Israeli occupation of the territory captured in the Six-Day War demanded military resources that stressed the IDF, requiring movement of facilities and more manpower. Although resented by the locals, the occupation saw little hostile resistance by residents as suggested by these lightly armed soldiers walking a patrol in a West Bank city. (IDF)

organisation, and planning. Anything in good shape and in high numbers, from mattresses to missiles, were adopted by the chronically cash-strapped Zahal. The greatly increased airspace benefitted IAF flight training. As months passed and diplomacy failed to find a path to resolution of the conflict, Israel began to settle in for a long stay. The army and intelligence services were stretched thin with the occupation.

Although the Israeli government proposed trading back most of the territories in exchange for peace treaties with its neighbours, military necessity required some establishment of installations in the areas. Yet, some of these appeared to exceed the security requirements of occupation. 'Hawks' pushed for expanding pseudo-permanent army infrastructure into the territories with camps and facilities moved into the West Bank especially.[3]

In occupation of Sinai the Israelis prepared for any further hostilities. Most of the land was impassable and of no significance. Roads were key militarily and so improved where necessary along with a substantial movement of infrastructure into the peninsula. With defences under Southern Command, orders came from Beersheba some 300km (185mi) from the canal. Sharm el-Sheikh, at the southern tip, was also considered vital as it commanded sea traffic in the area. Sinai's western shore, accessed via a narrow road along the southern coastline, was a jump-off point for Israeli operations against the Egyptian rear along the Gulf of Suez coast. The Egyptians saw it as a potential area to be seized given the slim IDF presence and difficulty in Israel rapidly enforcing same.

Months of work was required to 'clean up' the battlefields following the Six-Day War. Always hurting for funds, Zahal took the opportunity to adopt useful materiel left behind by the enemy. This Jordanian M-47 tank, being winched onto a trailer, was not adopted but nonetheless studied along with discovered paperwork and debriefings of POWs. (Albert Grandolini collection)

The occupation placed heavy demand on the IDF's transportation infrastructure. The rapid movement of priority personnel, especially across the vast Sinai Peninsula, demanded an inexpensive aircraft found in the Cessna U206 Stationair. It served liaison across the country and territories with ability to land on minimal airstrips in forward areas. This aircraft wears the emblem of 135 Squadron formed in 1974. (BIAF – Israel Aerospace Magazine)

For years Israeli and Egyptian soldiers peered at each other across the Suez Canal. Called the biggest antitank ditch in the world, the canal prevented easy mobile warfare, but shelling and small arms fire could be exchanged with ease. Fortifications grew in pace with the increasing volume of shelling. (Albert Grandolini collection)

The fly in that ointment was the superior Israel Air Force that would greatly impair any naval attacks and landings.

The IDF took over evacuated military installations in Sinai and altered them to their needs. The requirement to respond quickly to combat on the canal and exploit Sinai's strategic depth motivated the IAF to adopt evacuated Egyptian airfields. The former Bir Gifgafa AB, approximately 80km (50mi) from the canal, was renamed Refidim and hosted operations within weeks of the war. The Ras Nasrani airstrip at 'Sharm' was developed into a full airfield by August 1968 as Ophir. All were substantially expanded with fuel hydrant systems, underground command centres, and HAS. Bir Gifgafa was also the location of the IDF's major command centre in the south and a large field hospital was built on the base. Refidim became especially important for interceptors responding quickly to UARAF reconnaissance and strikes east of the waterway as well as rapid-response medical evacuation helicopters. Quick reaction alert was established there in March 1968, pilots in Mirage interceptor cockpits or nearby ready-rooms to launch rapidly. Squadrons rotated forward-deployed aircraft and personnel through these facilities. A pair of Mirages sat alert at Ophir after the UARAF stationed MiG-21s at Ghardaka AB (Hurgada), across the Red Sea. El Arish became a training base to take advantage of Sinai airspace, Fouga Magisters trainers moved there and students flown back and forth from Hatzerim AB near Beersheba.[4] Other former Egyptian airfields were maintained as emergency landing strips or air supply nodes. An entirely new airbase, Etzion, began to be built opposite Eilat – only the second such construction effort following Hatzerim in 1966–1967.

Israel built radar and air control stations atop Mount Tsafra in southern Sinai and Jebel Umm Rejem near Refidim. These complemented stations on Mount Aricha in the Negev and Mount Meron in northern Israel. All provided excellent tracking of opposition air traffic, except at very low altitude. The Hawk SAM radars likely came to serves as 'gap-fillers.' Air defence centres directed aerial engagements. The IDF established signals intelligence (SIGINT) and electronic intelligence (ELINT) 'listening posts' in the mountain passes east of the canal. The most significant of the former was at Jabal Umm Khisheb that the Israelis called Umm Hashiba.

Egyptian national assets lay within easy range of Israeli fighter-bombers while those of Israel were beyond reach of the UARAF – a reversal of pre-war circumstances.[5] Bombers based in Syria and Jordan could still reach vital Israeli assets just as quickly.

These were all remote and desolate locations slowly improved over the years from the initially dismal accommodations. Air force personnel were typically flown out to the bases and back again during their rotations on C-47 or Noratlas transports, or Arkia Inland Airlines commuters. The IAF pilots could also fly light planes to and from Israel, plus between bases within the small country. Senior Zahal personnel might be choppered to their posts. Aircrew would sit two-week alert rotations at Refidim with possible relief on weekends by reservists or emergency-posting pilots taking turns.[6] The duty was initially gruelling, with no cover and 90 minutes in the hot Mirage cockpit on hard seat packs, or freezing at night. Eventually shelters were built and sitting alert in the jet was reduced to 30 minutes. The later F-4Es' effective radar and missiles made it the choice for night alerts. Maintainers also had to learn to deal with dust storms affecting the aircraft.

The shallow Golan Heights required a semi-permanent military presence and fortifications were erected along with additional roads. Four SIGINT/ELINT posts were established on three tels (volcanic cones or hills) as well as on Mount Hermon (Jabal al-Shaykh). Hermon, at the northern end of the Heights, was the tallest peak in the area at 2,040m (6,690ft). Aside from visual surveillance, the radar station on the mountain gave exceptional ability to monitor Syrian air activity.

At first, life on the West Bank returned to relative normalcy. The Jordanian administrative infrastructure was retained and bridges to Jordan remained opened – with Israeli security checks. Palestinian irregulars infiltrated into the territory from Jordan in an effort to inspire inhabitants to rise up against their occupiers. However, the occupation was under the direction of Defence Minister Moshe Dayan who was inclined to allow the locals' lives to continue largely as before, with self-governance, relatively open borders and the benefits of access to Israeli markets, public services, and employment. The military presence was low-key, kept mostly away from the cities, and there was little violence. Consequently, the occupation was initially relatively benign although still resented.

Mount Hermon is the highest peak in the region and overlooks southern Syria, the Golan Heights, and south-eastern Lebanon. As such it is an ideal location for a military 'listening post' benefitting Israel who occupied the peak in June 1967, as well as visual observation as suggested by this image of an Zahal soldier defending one approach up the mountain. (IDF)

The IDF's electronic monitoring station on Tel Faris on the occupied Golan Heights shows the classical 'antenna farm' for such facilities. Similar installations elsewhere were vital elements in Israel's ability to hold the territories against Arab infiltration and provide general military intelligence collection. (David Nicolle)

The populace in the territories in large part wanted to be free of war, raise families, and have a fair chance at enjoying a good life. They began to experience the economic benefits of the occupation and many found work inside Israel. Within a few years half the wage earners were working in Israel and contributing substantially to a growth in the standard of living. This was despite pressure from the militants who insisted that this released Israelis for military duty. It certainly helped the Israeli economy that had been persistently limited by a shortage of labour.

Israeli citizens visited old sites from 19 years ago and locals began catering to these 'tourists.' Published maps soon showed the territories and Israel as one. There were also civil and emotional pressures to re-establish historical Jewish presence in some areas and gain assured access to holy sites. There were Israelis eager to move into Judea and Samaria to fulfil Zionist goals, belief in a 'Greater Israel', and religious fervour. The continuing conflict and lack of peace negotiations seemed to suggest a long period before hearts and minds would be changed, if not more blood spilled, to permit progress towards final settlement of the dispute. This removed some of the impediments to Israelis dwelling in the occupied territories, though of questionable legality.

Establishment of Jewish settlements and moving into Arab-dominated cities began within months of the war. People initially reoccupied settlements abandoned during 1948 fighting, to include within the Golan Heights and Gaza Strip, but soon extended to new settlements on land confiscated by Israel giving defence justification.[7] Some residents were evicted for military imperatives that suited settlement ends and in some cases existing structures were demolishing. Some of the settlers were Nahal paramilitary and the locations meant to support security purposes. Infrastructure was improved, lending the appearance of permanence. Running roads, power, telephone, and water to the settlements and facilities was costly and competed with other defence priorities in the budget. Much of this occurred without a clearly considered government policy and sometimes without approval. The government lacked resolve to oppose the settlements or remove the 'pioneers' and funded some of the activities. The Palestinians were justifiably incensed that land which they had owned for generations was being seized by a military administration allowing little legal recourse, adding to those from which they had been evicted in 1948.[8]

Anger towards the occupiers was sometimes expressed in demonstrations and civil disobedience. However, any signs of resistance would see the Israelis reveal that their velvet glove had a steel fist. They maintained the status quo with coercion and repression alternating with limited concessions and rewards. Shops involved in protest strikes would be forced open. When terror attacks surged there would be collective punishments such as curfews and movement restrictions together with systematic arrests, deportations, and homes demolitions. Between June 1967 and October 1969 some 7,000 homes of convicted terrorists or those who had supported them were reported demolished, affecting 50,000 people. Systematic arrest might include imprisonment and interrogation for long periods with some accusations of torture. Palestinians found guilty in Israeli courts of being members of, or supported, terrorist cells faced long jail terms while suspects were deported across the Jordan without trial.

In the few years following the war this Israeli migration into the territories did not assume the controversy and local resentment it would in later decades, but the seeds were sown. The settlers reasoned they could establish facts-on-the-ground to wait out any future policy decisions, and that public sympathy would fall on their side. Some in the military saw it as a means of securing defensible borders in any future negotiations because forcibly removing settlers would be exceedingly problematic. There were powerful organisations and cliques of citizenry who could not foresee giving back the whole of the West Bank and especially returning to a divided Jerusalem as part of any final resolution, and they moved to ensure any such effort would be so painful as to be politically untenable.

THE IMPASSE EMERGES

Many Arab nations were convinced of the 'Big Lie' that Western nations had contributed to Israel's military success in June 1967. The truth of the defeat was long coming to grips with and common citizens were seldom told the whole truth. For months diplomatic relations with Western countries were severed, the foreigners sent packing, and trade interrupted. Embassies in Baghdad, Damascus, and Cairo were shuttered, and others nations did likewise. The USA consulates in some Egyptian cities were sacked by mobs. The Americans were permitted only a small 'interest section' in Cairo. The Soviet Union closed its embassy in Israel and ordered Israel to do the same in the USSR. The Soviets also compelled most of the Eastern Bloc nations to sever relations with Israel. The Saudis, Libyans, and Kuwaitis were convinced to curtail crude oil deliveries to the USA, Western Europe, and Japan. Egyptian relations with the United Kingdom (UK, Great Britain) were re-established in October 1967 but doing the same with the USA remained too fraught. Nasser and other regional leaders would, over the coming years, continue painting the USA as the principal enemy of the Arab people. These attitudes and the diplomatic 'ghettos' impeded dialogue towards negotiation.

BLUE HELMETS

The fire incidents on the canal prompted the UN to negotiate a ceasefire in mid-July. This agreement was mediated by the Chief-of-Staff of the United Nations Truce Supervision Organization (UNTSO), Norwegian Lieutenant General Odd Bull.[9] The UNTSO was formed in 1948 to monitor the various truces negotiated during the Palestine war and later the armistice lines around Israel. This had been the UN's first peacekeeping mission, seeking to assist all parties in observing the terms of their mutual agreements and so monitored from the five contiguous states. Their observation posts (OP) shifted with the shifting battle lines over the decades. Then, with growing violence along the Suez Canal, the adversaries agreed to monitoring there, with Egypt on 10 July and Israel on the 11th. With a ceasefire in effect from the 15th, the 'blue helmet' observers began moving to establish OPs the next day. Ultimately, nine were emplaced along each side of the Suez Canal. On the Golan there were seven on the Israeli side of the line and nine in Syria. None were ever successfully negotiated for placements along the Jordan River or Lebanese fronts, especially as Fatah said that they would consider the foreign observers (all military officers) as hostiles.[10] However, three were added along the southern Lebanon border in spring 1972. Syria and Egypt refused to permit American peacekeepers on their soil or anyone who had served inside Israel.

Lieutenant General Odd Bull (right) of Norway, Chief-of-Staff of the United Nations Truce Supervision Organization, is seen in a meeting with the UN Secretary General U Thant at United Nations Headquarters on 14 June 1968. The UNTSO was established in the area after the 1948 war and soon established observation posts on the new ceasefire lines. It then became very active attempting to maintain the ceasefire and avoiding becoming casualties themselves as the fronts heated up, with even the Secretary General addressing relatively minor squabbles in an effort to prevent violence. (UN Photo)

The parties were consistently at odds over the most trivial issues and recalcitrant such that the UNTSO arbitration role was frustrating. Since the parties would not speak directly with each other, and restricted observer communications and travel across the ceasefire lines, all dialogue had to go through the UNTSO headquarters in Jerusalem. The Organization served as a communications conduit to the Security Council in New York where complaints about ceasefire violations were lodged and arbitrated – the Security Council having overseen negotiations for the June 1967 ceasefire. Even the Secretary General became involved in such minor parleys.

The UNTSO personnel recorded incidents, worked to resolve minor disputes, and tried to convince the armies to cease attacks when they occurred. This last was complicated in that commercial travel between the combatant nations was forbidden and had to be via a third country, though the UN flew its own aircraft directly (initially a C-47 Dakota then a Falcon 20). Even the most minor incident risked attacks. The observers came under fire themselves occasionally – sometimes clearly deliberately – becoming isolated and suffering casualties. Instead of observing compliance with terms of a ceasefire, they found themselves in an active war zone, risking life and limb. But, they remained. Some OPs had to be relocated and the local command centres moved back from area to avoid being hit.

Although leaders of the Arab combatant countries bore much responsibility for the catastrophic outcome of the war, especially in helping to trigger it, they all survived. They did this in part by blaming others and doubling-down on portraying the Jews as national and religious foes. Regardless, the fury at the defeat and humiliation in being made an international laughingstock was felt by most individuals throughout the Arab world. A fresh crop of Palestinian refugees deepened the sense of wrong to these people that many felt had to be rectified. Such feelings were not conducive to reconciliation. They caused a furore with determination to undo the 'aggression' and punish the perpetrator who was seen as continuing to impugn Arab dignity and deny the rights of the Palestinians. The leaders built upon this but, in doing so, came to limit their options for resolving the conflict.

The Israeli cabinet voted on 19 June 1967 to given back the occupied territories in return for direct negotiations with their Arab neighbours leading to peace treaties. Defence Minister Dayan famously said that he waited through the summer of 1967 for his phone to ring with Arab leaders ready to discuss an end to the imbroglio. This was not to be. Israel's opening was slapped away by the Arabs who were not in a good place for exploring options. Since Israel could never achieve a military victory by which she could impose an end to the conflict, the captured territories represented a new political element in offering to exchange land for peace. They did not wish to repeat the 1957 experience of withdrawing from Sinai, captured the previous year, with flimsy political guarantees. However, from the first some undefined territorial concessions to satisfy security imperatives were expected. These would be agreed through face-to-face peace negotiations. However, the Arabs would not sit down with Israel whom many considered an illegitimate state and who would be negotiating from a position of strength while the Arabs sat as the defeated. At best they needed an intermediary. Additionally, Israel was seized by feelings of relief and security it had never known, plus a sense they could accomplish anything enforced by praise from the world over. They felt no haste to return to the earlier situation and there was national consensus to hold the occupied land until circumstances permitted hammering out a final accord. Trading away this sense of security with the military buffer in some manner of agreement, with regimes that at best appeared untrustworthy or might be overthrown along with their agreements, would require security guarantees that few could imagine as unassailable given past experience. Israel would stand its ground until 'a just and lasting peace within secure borders' could be arrived at.

There were initially numerous proposals for a peace settlement. Israel suggested that the associated nations would agree to demilitarise the territories. Those countries saw this as infringing on their sovereignty and demanded Israel likewise demilitarise its border regions. Israel would be guaranteed passage through the Straits of Tiran and Suez Canal, though only in continuing to occupy Sharm el-Sheikh did the former seem certain. Israel would be recognised as a legitimate state with unimpeachable borders and normal relations established. Water resources were not to be impeded. Access to holy sites would be guaranteed though Israel insisted the unified Jerusalem would remain the capital of the state. Accommodations for Palestinian refugees would be pushed to beyond the initial peace treaty with the confrontation states. The Arabs insisted Israel withdraw to the 5 June 1967 frontiers as a precondition to any dialogue while Israel feared no talks would follow giving up its only bargaining chip. The Arabs would only consider declarations of non-belligerency and not a peace treaty with formal recognition. Suggested was partial implementation as a precondition or show of good faith. This would especially apply to forces withdrawing from immediately adjacent to the Suez Canal to permit its reopening. However, both sides feared this would become a semi-permanent and untenable situation.

Thus were the lines drawn. Months of debate followed the war on the world stage and in the UN General Assembly. At first the Arabs expected that, as in the aftermath of the Anglo-French-Israeli Suez Crisis of 1956, superpower and UN pressure would compel Israel to withdraw from the captured territories. They even demanded reparations for damage inflicted during the war. However, circumstances and political alignments were entirely different, especially given that Nasser had openly threatened war for months and brought together a coalition with the stated goal of wiping Israel off the map. No outside nation or organisation was inclined or likely could impose a solution to the conflict, even the superpowers. Even the June 1967 ceasefire held only while the combatants chose to respect it.

Throughout the months of nations talking *at* each other the Arabs felt they needed a united stand. A League of Arab States summit was held in Khartoum on 29 August through 1 September 1967 with 13 nations represented.[11] The League issued a declaration on the 1st stating that there would be 'no peace with Israel, no recognition of Israel, no negotiations with it', and added 'insistence on the rights of the Palestinian people in their own country.' Notable was that the declaration did not call for the eradication of the 'Zionist entity', appearing to accept that Israel was permanent. Although assenting to coordinate on joint responses to the crises, there was otherwise no firm decisions on how to proceed. Agreement was reached for Saudi Arabia, Kuwait, and Libya to provided $378 million quarterly to Egypt and Jordan as compensation for lost revenue from canal transit fees, Sinai oil fields, and tourism. (Syria boycotted the summit and so was excluded from the largess.) These monies would assist in reconstituting armed forces. To help pay these grants, there was also a decision to lift the oil embargo that had proven largely ineffectual aside from impacting revenue to the producers.

Nasser led the increasing Arab animosity against Israel. He moved to isolate Israel politically and economically, increasing the cost of the occupation. The Arab League expanded the long-standing Arab Boycott and compelled many emergent countries, who had previously welcomed Israeli assistance, to distance themselves from the country. Arab states were able to rally especially developing third world and 'nonaligned' nations behind their efforts to segregate Israel and paint her as colonialist and imperialist. These nations assisted in forming an anti-Israeli voting bloc in the UN. Debates and resolutions from the UN more and more condemned Israel and chastised her defence actions. Israel came to view the General Assembly as largely one-sided and anti-Israel, and denounced most of its pronouncements. These eventually became meaningless 'noise' that contributed only resentment within Israel and a growing determination to stand her ground. Yet, seen as the occupier of land and people gained by war and perpetuating the Palestinian diaspora, Israel was successfully anointed an international pariah. This was hardly a unified front for many Arab leaders distrusted Nasser or had grievances with others.

Debate had continued in the UN and the Security Council passed Resolution 242 on 22 November 1967 as the basis for resolving the conflict. This opened with a general statement recognising the 'inadmissibility of the acquisition of territory by war.' It then called for Israeli withdrawal 'from territories occupied in the recent conflict.' Focusing on this aspect and the lack of a call for peace treaties,

Egypt accepted the Resolution on 23 November and Jordan soon after. Syria, Iraq and Saudi Arabia rejected it. Having assured that the document did not explicitly call for withdrawal from *all* territories, Israel nominally accepted the Resolution on 1 May 1968.[12]

While Resolution 242 appeared a step forward, its implementation would be daunting. To Israeli reading it left open the potential for adjustments of the 1949 boundaries and acceptance of those borders as inviolate – tacit recognition of Israel's right to exist. To the Arabs the Khartoum declaration closed off any negotiations, leaving only Israeli withdrawal and return to the pre-war situation as the goal. Additionally, Nasser pronounced on 23 November 1967 that 'whatever is taken by force cannot be restored except by force', indicating he considered hostilities as the only course of action should Israel continue to stall withdrawal. The belligerent rhetoric, from the supposed leader of the Arab world, left him and the other nations few options but hostilities. While at least ambassadors and foreign ministers continued to talk, Nasser privately made clear this was a stalling tactic until a military solution could be enacted. At a minimum, realisation they could be pushed out of the territories would induce Israel to adopt more amenable negotiating positions.

With the Khartoum 'Three Noes' and talk of war, Israel saw that there would be no quick resolution. As the months passed, with the IDF settling into the territories and civilians establishing residences, the opportunities for a settlement became ever more difficult. Hardliners began taking the initiative and any perceived middle ground shrank. In Israel these people could not foresee returning all of the territories but even defining acceptable border adjustments was too fraught politically. Their views began to make compromise politically unpalatable.

Breaking out of the basic proposed negotiating positions to determine agreeable compromises, and even getting the parties talking, became the stuff of high diplomacy occupying the time of leaders the world over. Effectively left out were the Palestinians whose voice was always strident, had no representation of their own, and were manipulated by the Arab states.

The UN Secretary General appointed a special envoy, Dr Gunnar Jarring, Sweden's ambassador to the USSR, to work with the combatant nations towards implementation of 242. Jarring held numerous meetings within the UN and travelled extensively throughout the region. The first set of formal talks went on for five weeks with the UN ambassadors of Israel, Egypt, Jordan, and Lebanon – with Syria and Iraq declining to participate. These made no progress. Consequently, Jarring's missions proved largely fruitless and were suspended in early 1969.

4

AN UNEASY CEASEFIRE

Emboldened by the new equipment supplied by the USSR, Egypt and Syria especially kept the borders hot with artillery barrages, commando raids, airstrikes, and sponsored Palestinian insurgency. The thirst for vengeance and recovery of occupied land was widespread. Yet, the armed forces of these countries had to be rehabilitated and grown if they were to reengage the Israelis, and this took time. Restoring their airpower was the first priority given the deep losses and need to confront any Israeli renewal of its bombing. Palestinian irregulars were largely ready and became more active than ever in harassing Israel. The Soviet Union also wished to increase its presence in the region, support her associates and see them succeed with Soviet weapons and tactics, punishing Israeli 'aggression' to the detriment of the enabling 'Western imperialists' from the perspective of the Cold War. An armed conflict of increasing intensity developed on Israel's borders and then the international stage. It all became 'the war after the war' with 'peacetime' military engagements on all sides unlike anything these nations had experienced previously. There was high potential for it escalating further and sparking another general war. Injecting aspects of nationalism, religious zeal, and racism, the conflict appeared endless and undermining the national ideals of all parties with hatred and bloodshed.

HEATING-UP THE SUEZ

Immediately following the war Egypt blocked the Suez Canal, a waterway of immense importance for international commerce and the movement of warships, by scuttling several vessels and sinking concrete-filled floating docks at several points. This was a move to compel international pressure for Israel to withdraw. In the coming months, as the area became a zone of continuing military action, it became unsafe to reopen the canal.[1] The closure was sorely felt by shippers and navies worldwide but they adjusted over time.[2] This only drove Egypt to consider military action as the avenue to keep the conflict in the world's consciousness.

Tensions remained high along the canal following the ceasefire and increased when Egyptian observers reported an Israeli armoured brigade moving toward El Qantarah. A canal crossing was feared and Nasser authorised an airstrike. Fog prevented the aircraft taking off and, in the nervous interim, observers realised the Israelis were merely reinforcing their positions. Nasser cancelled the airstrike and his forces stood down.[3]

Israeli leadership had decided that holding a defensive line at the 160km (100mi) long east bank of the canal, and along the gulf, was the least costly and most politically acceptable. They feared any success by Egypt in gaining a foothold in Sinai might become permanent under a UN-sponsored ceasefire and erode Israel's bargaining power or serve as a springboard for a full offensive to retake the peninsula. The IDF dug in and regular elements of the army were stationed in Sinai's western plain to deter Egyptian crossing of the canal and to respond if they did. The decision by Jerusalem to remain defensive as the front heated up sacrificed the IDF's traditional mobile warfare strengths. Any armoured incursion on the west bank implied a major amphibious operation across formidable water obstacles and significant international repercussions. However, holding the line stressed resources given the small regular forces.

While the disposition of IDF elements right at the water's edge made a statement of full control of the peninsula it also placed troops at risk. Egyptian and Israeli troops were within ready range of direct and indirect fire plus quick airstrikes. With the waterway between 60 and 110m (195 and 360ft) across in the straight sections, bullets could be exchanged as easily as harsh language.

As with Israel, the canal inhibited decisive means of Egypt engaging the IDF in Sinai. President Nasser felt that some semblance of victories against the enemy would restore morale and hearten the populace. He called for the army to inflict five Israeli casualties per day. Consequently, the UAR began low-level military action harassing the IDF as soon as her forces were properly ensconced along the front and reequipped. The Israelis responded as they could, trying to compel a return to the ceasefire and forestall an Egyptian campaign across the canal. As was her wont, Israeli reprisals were disproportionate to the incitement.

Israeli artillery rounds are seen impacting the west bank of the Suez Canal, at left, likely across the wide Great Bitter Lake that had 14 stranded vessels at anchor (another in Lake Timsah). Even at this point on the watercourse, like that at right, commandos could paddle across in rubber dinghies to carry out reconnaissance or sabotage operations. (IDF)

Just a week or so following the war Egyptians began occasional sniping and shelling of Israelis seen on the eastern bank. Any movement of personnel and vehicles could draw fire. The first IDF fatality was on 15 June. The Israelis were limited by manpower to a presence at specific locations along the canal and vehicle patrols between. This left opportunities for Egyptian infiltration. The UARAF flew reconnaissance over the east bank and lost their first aircraft to defences on 4 July.

Among the initial fire exchanges on the canal were those prompted by each nation asserting its perceived prerogative to operate on the waterway. The June 1967 ceasefire did not detail such privileges. The Egyptians held that the ceasefire line ran along the east bank while Israel insisted it ran down the middle of the canal. After Egyptians put boats into the water Dayan ordered that the IDF to do the same. They paddled out rubber dinghies displaying large national ensigns as a literal 'show the flag' display of Israeli possession of Egyptian sovereign territory. The Egyptians did likewise as a show of defiance. The first such Zahal show on 14 July was met with gunfire that sank the craft. On that day Dayan met the UNTSO's General Bull to state that either both sides should use the Suez Canal or none. Egypt wanted to open the canal but the Israelis demanded a share of the royalties which Cairo rejected. On 17 July Cairo Radio announced that the presence of an Israeli ship in the canal would be regarded as a breach of the ceasefire and met with appropriate force. From that point, whenever the opposition put a dinghy in the water, it was fired upon. Two Israel Navy personnel ended up in Egyptian custody during one such incident. The small arms exchanges escalated to tank duels, artillery shelling, then fighter jets, before subsiding … until the next incident. This 'Dinghy War', with Israel suffering nine deaths and 55 injured, continued for a few weeks before an agreement, negotiated via the UNTSO, on non-navigation of the canal was reached on 3 August. Neither side was permitted to use the canal and so it remained closed indefinitely.

Israel chose to defend the captured Sinai Peninsula directly on the east bank of the Suez Canal. This required observation posts and patrols that became targets for Egyptian sniping, shelling and commando forays. Even after hardened forts were built along the length of the canal the patrols between were continued, usually looking like this with a few infantrymen (commonly reservists on their annual duty) in a lightly armoured halftrack. These vehicles are probably on the unpaved track north of Qantarah with the sand berm to their right. (IDF)

Three weeks after the end of the war there was action in the swampy area to the south of Port Fuad, on the west bank opposite Port Said and at the northern entrance to the Suez Canal. The area to 9km (6mi) south had remained under Egyptian control and held little military significance. In the conflicting accounts General Ismail Ali claimed to have sent a company of 100 soldiers in boats to the east bank on 1 July under the cover of shelling from the west bank and warships in the harbours. These repelled an Israeli attempt to occupy the area, knocking out six tanks and inflicting casualties. The IDF claim to have sent an armoured patrol along the narrow causeway paralleling the canal against two Egyptian platoons that had crossed in boats, moving south to near the hamlet of Ras el-Ush, 12–15km (7–9mi) south of Port Fuad, in an effort to expand the zone. The column came under tank and artillery fire from across the waterway. With inability to manoeuvre on the causeway the IDF force pushed ahead but met stiff resistance that knocked out vehicles and left 14 dead including the company commander. The Israelis pulled back the next day but continued to probe the area and take fire. It was during this spasm of violence that Egypt performed her first commando raid east of the canal, as early as 3 July, and their first airstrike on the 5th.

Left: The Su-7 remained among the Arab strike aircraft working on Israel's northern and southern fronts. It had several grave deficiencies but the Soviets had little better to offer or willing to supply. (David Nicolle collection)

Centre: The first IAF aircraft loss following the war a Mirage and the fleet was slowly attrited over the coming years of combat and training. This image shows the remains of a Mirage in the desert sand as imaged by the Su-7BMK shooting the photo in 1969. Israel had good success with ejection seats and recovering her downed personnel. (EAF)

A few days of this back-and-forth with mutual casualties brought artillery barrages on the 8th extending south to the El Qantarah area. This caught the IDF ill-prepared and they suffered additional personnel losses. Reaction extended to IAF airstrikes and an air battle developed on 8 July as the UARAF responded. A Mirage knocked down a MiG-21. A Su-7 was brought down by ground fire during attacks in the Qantarah area on the 11th and the pilot, the squadron commander, succeeded in evading capture and swimming across the canal.

It was 12 July before the Israelis felt they had stabilised the situation near Port Fuad, choosing to contain the unimportant area. It remained the only portion of Sinai held by Egypt and so the 'Battle of Ras el-Ush' was heralded within the armed forces as the first success against the IDF following the war.

Vessels transporting and replenishing special operations (specops) teams on opposition shores were occasionally discovered and engaged. During a patrol on the night of 11/12 July 1967 the destroyer INS *Eilat* (K40) and two Ayah-class MTBs, T-203 and T-204 *Ayah* and *Daya*, discovered two Egyptian P-6 MTBs off the northern Sinai coast, opposite Romani. In deciding to engage the Egyptian craft the Israelis chose to use *Eilat* as bait while the smaller boats hid in the radar shadow of the coastline.[4] The P-6s rushed at the destroyer but launched their torpedoes too early and they were easily evaded by *Eilat*. *Ayah* and *Daya* then joined the battle, chasing one of the P-6s west until finally sinking it with its 20mm deck guns. One of the IN boat's crew struggled to reload their gun, having to withdraw several times. *Eilat* fired multiple 40mm rounds into the

The MiG-21F-13 from the war had many advantages over later models to include a powerful internal gun and some manoeuvre benefits. In the hands of a capable pilot it could give Israeli interceptors a hard time. However, its disadvantages and many inexperienced pilots made the MiG quite vulnerable to skilled Israelis in their Mirages. (Reda el-Iraqi collection)

NAVAL DISPARITY

The Egyptian Navy was the best equipped of the region with 14 destroyers, frigates, and corvettes, eight minesweepers, 44 patrol boats, 13 submarines, 21 landing craft, and dozens of other torpedo boats, gun boats, and support vessels. New to naval warfare were 18 Soviet Komar (Mosquito) and larger Osa (Wasp) class fast attack craft – missile (FAC(M)) with the P-15 Termit (Termite) surface-to-surface missiles (SSM). Egypt possessed good port facilities, but crews were of questionable proficiency. Perhaps 50 percent of the force was not combat-ready. Two frigates and four motor torpedo boats (MTB) were also trapped in the blocked canal. Loss of movement through the Suez Canal was a significant operational impediment. The USSR might also come to Egypt's defence with its Mediterranean fleet. The Syrian navy was considerably smaller, made up primarily of coastal patrol craft, antisubmarine vessels, and 10 Komars recently received from the USSR.

The nations confronting Israel funded creation of the Palestine Arab Navy in 1967. Operating from Lebanon, it began collecting small craft and trained for smuggling personnel and weapons into the Gaza Strip and terror forays against the Israeli coast plus across the Dead Sea. The Israel Navy (IN) had to patrol the coast persistently to monitor traffic which might be bringing raiding parties or arms to fedayeen in the Strip. There were 56 small craft intrusions recorded between October 1971 and October 1973.[5]

The top image is an Osa I missile boat with four missile launchers and below is a Komar-class FAC(M) with two, firing a Termit anti-ship missile. These boats and their missiles were new to naval warfare and as yet unproven when introduced to the Egyptian and Syrian navies. Little was known about the Termit system in the West, yet the Israeli navy was trying to address the threat. (Public Domain and Albert Grandolini collection)

As part of the preparation for the next war with Israel, the Egyptian Navy spent more time at sea training and in support of ground forces. Soviet naval presence increased and advisors were evidently aboard every ship sailing for training and combat. Egypt joined the USSR in training exercises. Its berths in Suez and Port Said were within IDF artillery range. Ports on the Red Sea coast were initially poor until improved. Port Sudan became available following the September 1969 coup in that country. Vessels were upgraded in Pakistan and India. Coastal artillery was also moved under navy responsibility. The ageing Il-28 bombers were employed in sea patrol missions.

The IN had always been on the short end of the budgetary stick at less than 10 percent of outlays. It was, consequently, a poor outfit with outdated vessels usually at a low state of readiness and with marginally trained crews. The air force augmented the navy to ensure sufficient patrol and attack capabilities, though as a secondary or tertiary role. By summer 1967 the IN was in a transitional phase, with older ships docked to help pay for newer yet to arrive. Operational vessels were one submarine, one destroyer, five torpedo boats, and a few landing craft. With little effective offensive capability, the IN was principally expected to protect the coast from enemy bombardment from the sea and prevent attacks on shipping. As the economy improved following the war and the

An Israel Navy FAC(T) patrol boat, the IN T503 *Tarshish*, patrols the Sinai coast in the late 1960s. These patrols were important to prevent infiltration of special forces and smuggling of arms to militants in the occupied territories. One of three Ophir-class craft which were obtained from Italy in 1957, the boats were long-in-tooth and replaced in the early 1970s with the Dabur-class. The torpedo tubes and 40mm gun have been removed, retaining only the two 20mm guns. (IDF)

defence budget grew the IN acquired additional vessels. A series of coastal patrol boats were bought from Japan and the USA, plus built in Israel. A few large ships suitable for transport and landing commandos were commissioned, pushing aside the older and decrepit fleet. Amphibious capabilities were also plused-up, to include accommodating tanks and even helicopters, if needed.

Israel possessed a small fleet of landing craft and had prepared for a landing during the Six-Day War, though ultimately cancelled. These represented the only, albeit modest, means of taking a war of movement into Egyptian territory west of the Suez Canal via operations on the Mediterranean or Gulf of Suez coasts. Here INS *Ashdod*, P-61, practices landing a captured T-55 tank during training in the late 1960s. (Ilan Warshai collection)

Israel established a naval presence on the Sinai coast at Sharm el-Sheikh and Ras Sudr while undertaking routine and boring patrols of the coastline and into the Red Sea. Coastlines to patrol had increased four-fold to 486nm versus an original 109nm (not counting the 54nm of the Dead Sea, expanded from 29nm). This also included the Egyptian oil drilling and loading facilities at Belayim, off Abu Rodeis on the Gulf of Suez, which the Israelis would begin working.[6] Hence, operations were extended farther afield than ever before while new vessels were only slowly arriving.

The Termit missiles on the Egyptian and Syrian FAC(M)s were the greatest IN worry. This was the export version of the SS-N-2 'Styx' (per NATO classification) active-homing radar-guided missiles. It was a 2,340kg (5,160lb) missile with a 500kg (1,000lb) warhead and a range of 40km (25mi). This represented a new naval threat. Instead of firing scores of shells to hit an enemy vessel, a single missile could cripple or sink a warship many times the size of the attacker and at greater range. Little was known in the West about the Termit but the Israelis assumed that the Arab navies were too inept to employ them effectively. Nonetheless, the IN installed radar detection gear (Electronic Support Measures, ESM) and chaff rockets aboard some ships to help address the threat.

Israel's Gabriel surface-to-surface anti-ship missile is seen in a test shot off a boat at sea. It was more advanced than the Soviet Termit missiles being delivered to the Arab navies but of shorter range and smaller warhead. Yet, the missile and the boats that would carry them were essential in modernising the Israel Navy. If this program failed the service could well be disbanded. (Ron Feldman collection)

Israel had already developed their own SSM in the Gabriel. This 430kg (950lb) missile was guided initially via shipboard radar, skimming just a few metres above the water, until acquiring the target with its own radar for terminal guidance. It possessed a 100kg (220lb) warhead and 20km (12mi) range. The country had ordered a dozen Sa'ar (Storm) FAC(M)s from France (though a German hull) to be armed with this weapon. Deliveries of the boats were to begin in 1969. The Sa'ar would form the backbone of the modernised Israel Navy in a gamble that, if it failed, could be the death knell for the service that had theretofore appeared virtually superfluous.

other vessel, approaching to 40m (130ft), until it was dead in the water then exploded. Eight sailors on the Israeli ship were hurt by flying debris that also caused some damage. All of the Egyptian crewmen from both boats died. The gunners had been unable to bring the ship's main 4.5-inch gun to bear because the crew found they could not remove the safety wire from shell fuses. Hence, poor training and inadequate proficiency was evident in the chaotic battle. Furthermore, the Israelis could be accused of breaching the ceasefire in luring the Egyptian boats to fight (who fired first) and then pursuing them into Egyptian national waters. The Egyptians sought an opportunity to deliver a similar loss to the Israelis.

Egypt's first heavy shelling occurred on the 14 July and cost the Israelis 64 casualties with nine dead. Israeli airstrikes on the 15th and a photo-reconnaissance (PR) run along the canal to determine Egyptian artillery battery dispositions, with the UARAF doing the same, resulted in another aerial duel. Egypt lost five more jets, one becoming the first success for Israel's Dragonfly (Shafrir) air-to-air missile (AAM), while a Mirage was lost to a Soviet R-3S AAM in the bargain. Artillery exchanges grumbled on into September. The Egyptian garrison on Green Island (Jazirat al-Akh'dah), 4km (3mi) south of Suez City, helped direct shells on positions along the southern part of the canal and also engaged Israeli landing craft on resupply missions along the coast. The front grew quiet for a few weeks with the help of UN mediation and pressure from superpowers. The IDF continued to suffer casualties from sporadic shelling until the attacks petered out in early October. The lull was possibly due in part to the Egyptians running short of ammunition but also because their gunners were firing blind owing to lack of a suitable photo-reconnaissance capability by the air force.

With imminent deployment of UN observers along the canal the IDF hastily took control of 18 outposts on 15 July that were each manned with just a few soldiers and backed up with tanks. These lay along the waterway covering the approaches to the inland roads and where the canal joined the lakes that interrupted its course. Although fortified with sandbags and corrugated steel sheets, such protection extended only to small arms and light mortar fire. Following the heavy shelling events, plans were laid for more suitable positions. This proposed a series of fortifications, each housing approximately a company of soldiers and supporting an enormous vehicle park. This bespoke a much larger commitment of personnel and armoured vehicles than the government felt it could sustain. Ultimately, only a few bunkers were constructed, and the overall plan went unimplemented.[7] This meant IDF elements remained vulnerable to artillery fire that had to be suppressed via counter-battery fire and airstrikes.

The IDF's defence of the Suez front was underpinned by the active 7th Armoured Brigade. Most of the reserve troops who spent the early summer overlooking the waterway in 1967 were demobilised from August and replaced by the 275th Territorial Infantry Brigade using reserve troops on rota augmented by active elements of the army. The southern region was held by the new 72nd Territorial Infantry Brigade, a similar formation, but largely infantry augmented by active paratrooper and reconnaissance companies. Until 1969 the IDF held Sinai with perhaps 15,000 soldiers, sailors and airmen including 15 percent of the active army of whom a few thousand were stationed on the canal. This was a boring routine for the average soldier who travelled 10–12 hours from their bases in Israel in buses without air conditioning over bad roads. They lived with only canvas sheets as protection from the searing heat of the sun in daylight, the bitter cold of the night, and frequent choking sand storms at any time of the day. For their commanders it was difficult to keep them busy and maintain morale. To protect their positions they built wire entanglements and laid minefields while conducting foot and vehicle patrols along the waterway. In off-duty moments they sometimes fished and shouted across the water to their counterparts on the opposite bank. Impromptu games of football gave a brief opportunity to let off steam.

A refurbished diesel-electric submarine, the INS *Dakar* (Swordfish), sailing from the UK, went missing during its transit to Israel in January 1968 with its crew of 69. An extensive search failed to locate any trace of the sub. Speculation included attack by the Egyptians.[8] Combined with the *Eilat* sinking (next page) and operational accidents, the Israel Navy lost 10 percent of its sailors and a third of its submariners within the span of three months.

Egyptians were greatly cheered by the *Eilat* sinking. Israel retaliated on the 24th with shelling of Suez and Port Tawfiq for three hours. The harbour and fertiliser plant were hit then oil refineries and petrochemical facilities set ablaze. The refinery had manufactured all of Egypt's heating and cooking gas, and supplied 77 percent of its refined oil. There was $164 million in damage and lost product plus introducing a paraffin shortage. Given the IDF's meagre retaliatory means, attacking such infrastructure targets raised the level of national 'pain' while Egypt could do little of the

Israel retaliated for the *Eilat* sinking by shelling the refinery and oil storage in Suez on 24 October 1967 (likely photographed from an Israeli artillery spotter airplane). The city and its facilities would be hit by ground and air attack many more times over the coming three years, along with other canal cities. These became battered ghost towns, evacuated of all but minimum essential inhabitants and military personnel. (IAF)

DEATH OF A DESTROYER

The IN patrols off Sinai's northern coast extended past the canal entrance to Port Said – for no evident reason other than to 'thumb their noses' at the Egyptians. Frustrated by this, Egypt planned an 'ambush' as the Israelis would call it. At dusk on 21 October the destroyer *Eilat*, flagship of the Israel Navy, approach the harbour for its turn, 22km (13.5mi) off the coast. (Territorial waters extend to 19km/12mi and Egypt insisted *Eilat* was just inside this limit.) It was engaged by two P-15 missiles fired from Komar TP-501, under Commander Lutfi Jadallah, off the breakwater of the port. The first inkling of danger was when the destroyer's lookouts saw the flame and smoke from the missile's rocket booster. The captain, Lieutenant Commander Yitzhak Shoshan, immediately changed course to reduce his radar cross section by presenting the destroyer's stern to the missile's radar sensor while the anti-aircraft gunners tried to engage with their 40mm Bofors and 20mm Oerlikon guns. The manoeuvres appeared successful for the missile passed 6nm astern before its on-board radar re-acquired the target. The P-15 swung around and struck the destroyer on the stern, stalling the engines and knocking out the radio. A second missile struck amidships leaving *Eilat* ablaze, listing and unable to manoeuvre.

Damage-control parties went to work and despite dense smoke fought the fires for 90 minutes, hoping to remain afloat until rescue. A missile from Komar TP-504, under Commander Ahmed Shaker, then penetrated the magazine causing a detonation that rendered the fires uncontrollable.[9] After another 15 minutes Captain Shoshan ordered abandon ship. The destroyer soon slid beneath the waves. A fourth Termit struck amongst survivors in the water.

A radio had been improvised aboard the badly damaged ship and the message relayed via an army post ashore two hours after the initial attack. Still, rescue operations were slow getting started owing to miscommunication. The first aircraft was overhead an hour after the ship went under. After dark, Mirage pilots used their radar to locate the site and guide others in repeatedly ejecting flares to illuminate the rescue area. Noratlas transports dropped inflatable rafts to the seamen until Super Frelon and S-58 helicopters began hoisting sailors aboard, and finally navy ships arrived. Of the 199 men aboard *Eilat*, 31 were killed, 16 missing and believed dead, and more than 91 wounded. Between January and February 1968, Israeli divers blew up the wreck that was in 10–12 fathoms of water. The Egyptian Navy dived on the debris seeking classified equipment and documents. They recovered six bodies which were returned to Israel through the Red Cross.

The navy had intelligence that the Egyptians were planning some action but had not communicated this to Shoshan who was the service's SSM and ESM expert. The experienced operators of the Bat Kol ESM gear had been left ashore for training and there is conflicting information regarding whether the system was manned at the time of the attack. The effectiveness of this new system, that provided bearing but not range, was unknown. It required a highly skilled operator to correlate SIGINT data on the missile threat from ship sensors and compare them with printed data manuals. Any on-watch operator aboard *Eilat* was likely uncertain what he was observing. Though sought by the underfunded navy, chaff rockets were evidently not available. The wisdom of 'showing the flag' by trooping in front of the Egyptians, as ordered by Dayan, appeared ill-advised given the IN's glaring operational weaknesses. Gross failures of command and operational errors were evident in the tragedy, but no immediate changes were made.

The first warship destroyed in combat by missile, the sinking of *Eilat* proved one of major events which shaped naval warfare during the twentieth century. It attracted keen attention of navies across the globe.

The Israeli destroyer INS *Eilat* is seen in happier times prior to its sinking on 21 October 1967. It was hit by Termit missiles fired from Egyptian Komar boats just outside Alexandria harbour, becoming the first warship to be sunk in combat by surface-to-surface missile. The loss of life may have been heavier but for rescue efforts assisted by the IAF. (IDF)

same. The IAF also attacked Egyptian missile boats in the ports of Alexandria and Port Said. Soviet vessels had been present until a few days prior but quickly returned and remained a persistent presence to discourage Israeli strikes, believing she would not risk accidentally hitting USSR warships.

Artillery exchanges then erupted along the length of the front. Zahal shelling included targeting fire sources from within the cities on the west bank of the canal (Suez, Ismailia and Qantarah), killing and wounding hundreds of people along with extensive property damage.[10] The canal cities had held nearly a million inhabitants pre-war who had relied upon transit directly or indirectly for their livelihood. That gone and facing Israeli guns on the opposite bank they had begun drifting away – about 100,000 soon after the war. The shelling during July prompted tens of thousands more to flee. In September Nasser ordered a stand-down to enable evacuations of Suez and Ismailia, and quiet again settled along the waterway. By October 60 percent of inhabitants had gone, mostly women, the young and the old. The relocations creating an enormous internal refugee problem. This was obvious to most as 'clearing the decks' in preparation of renewed hostilities as much as for civilian safety.

A period of relative calm followed apart from the occasional exchange of artillery fire, patrols and the odd air clash. The Israelis appear to have believed they had cowed their enemies into submission. The Egyptian Army built fortified positions offering more safety from enemy shelling.

THE NORTHERN FRONT

Syria only cautiously engaged the IDF and confined themselves to low-level harassment as it had in the past, but now on the Golan Heights. The first action was on 15 July 1967 when SyAAF MiG-21s flew aggressively towards the ceasefire line. The IAF responded and lost an aircraft to a mishap. Shelling, Katyusha rocketing, tank fire and terror attacks continued through 1968 at a steady pace from Syrian forces and irregulars. The initial ground actions were guerrilla raids that brought the expected Zahal reaction. Cross-border forays began with an attack in December 1967.

Syria hosted a number of Palestinian military groups, especially the PLA and Fatah, the latter with four training camps near Damascus. Although encouraged to attack Israel, these groups were all carefully regulated by the Syrian Arab Army much to the frustration of the militants. The PLA's Hittin Brigade eventually had eight battalions and 12,000 men but was riven by disputes, underarmed and underfunded by its patron, and more of a showpiece for parades than a genuine fighting force. Along with Palestinian units integrated into the army, Syria created in spring 1968 the Thunderbolt (al-Saiqa) strike force. As the Israelis responded to provocations the Syrians also directed Saiqa commandos to strike from Lebanon.

The clamour following the Six-Day War brought calls from the Moslem majority in Lebanon for the country to join the pushback against Israel while the Christian community wanted it to remain neutral. Guerrilla activity from Lebanon gradually grew to include shelling of Israel's northern settlements, mining of roads and agricultural fields, and attacks on IDF patrols. The first cross-border infiltration was on 4 January 1968 and guerrilla activity ramped up from there. The attacks brought Israeli retaliation or pre-emptive operations ahead of terrorist incursions, including airstrikes, while also building bomb shelters for border communities.

It was clear the potential for increasing guerrilla and conventional attacks in the north was high.

JORDANIAN CONUNDRUM

Transjordan was created in 1920 by separating into two the portion of the Levant mandated to Great Britain for oversight by the League of Nations. Palestine lay west of the Jordan River and Transjordan east of the river.[11] Abdullah bin al-Hussein of the House of Hasim (Hashemites), rulers of Mecca, was put in place by the British in 1921 to govern the region as Amir. Transjordan was granted independence by Britain in 1946 whereupon Hussein was declared King. The country was renamed the Hashemite Kingdom of Jordan in 1949.

Essentially foreigners installed by a colonial power, the Husseins were always careful to placate internal parties in the tribal country. To these were added many more Palestinians in 1948 via refugees and Jordan's occupation of the region of Palestine west of the river. This Jordan annexed in 1950. The international community largely considered the annexation as illegal and Arab nations viewed it as essentially holding the area 'in trust' until the Palestinian issue was resolved. The district was largely populated by Palestinians who were granted Jordanian citizenship with full commensurate rights and privileges. With the other Palestinians in the country, they made up more than half of Jordan's two million inhabitants and had representation amongst the nation's leadership. However, as many Palestinians saw the West Bank as an element of a future state, the annexation was not looked upon kindly. They painted the Hashemites as illegitimate rulers, emplaced by imperialists, on land historically inhabited by Palestinian Arabs. King Abdullah was assassinated at the Al-Aqsa Mosque in Jerusalem during 1951 by a Palestinian who feared the monarch was preparing to make peace with Israel. Hence, Jordan was especially firm with Palestinian groups in the West Bank to suppress national aspirations that might contest Jordanian domination of the area.

Jordan could not but back the Arab Street move to isolate Israel without negotiation. Always fearful of challenges to their rein, the Husseins had been loath to join formal alliances. The third King, Hussein bin Talal crowned in 1952, felt compelled to join the move towards war in May 1967. Initially standing on the side-lines, he was beset with criticism by the wider Arab press and leaders while the army's morale flagged. When he did move the war proved disastrous with loss of the West Bank and the armed forces left seriously tattered under Egyptian command. There was, consequently, great reluctance to become part of another coalition challenging Israel. In March 1969 an Arab Eastern Command was nominally created by Jordan, Syria, and Iraq but it was another desert mirage. Within months the dedicated forces were reassigned.

Hussein had several secret contacts with Israeli officials into the autumn of 1968. When he explored potential diplomatic solutions he received only vague proposals and saw a hardening of the Israeli position. Like other Arab leaders he was disappointed the Americans seemed to do nothing to soften the Israeli stand. There was no way Hussein would survive any unilateral peace agreement between Jordan and Israel.

The King had no intention of challenging Israel in a manner that would incite retaliatory strikes and possible incursions to seize buffer territory. However, the war had weakened the state's ability to control the militants operating from its territory, especially as the Palestinians flooding across the border included fighters. Egypt armed and trained the 141st Palestinian Fedayeen Battalion that operated from a base near Amman.[12] Syria guided fighters across the border into the country. Jordan inevitably became a very active battleground in the Arab-Israeli conflict during 1967–1970.

The fedayeen sought to use the confusion immediately following the war to infiltrate guerrilla squads into the West Bank and Gaza Strip to foment revolution against the occupier and launch attacks inside the territories and Israel. Consequently, Fatah was to enable thousands of guerrillas, operating from Jordan, to cross the river on raids and then return to east bank sanctuaries. Jordan became the principal base of PLO actions and Fatah headquarters was moved from Damascus to Amman on 6 February 1968. This got Fatah out from under the control of the Syrian Army and so permitted more freedom of action.

In anticipation of a 'popular rebellion', Fatah began to create clandestine cells in West Bank villages. Arafat is reported to have operated in the region between July and September 1967. However, these were essentially reception centres for fedayeen who had avoided the Israeli security forces. They sought to link up with comrades in the occupied territory, smuggle arms, or undertake terror actions. Although the infiltrators found some welcome among the populace, there was little enthusiasm for launching a mass armed revolt. These forays extended along the roughly 167km (104mi) or so frontier from Lake Kinneret to the Dead Sea, and from the Arava valleys further south to Aqaba. The Israelis hunted the infiltrators while punishing the Jordanians. The IDF also erected barriers, laid minefields, established outposts, and instituted patrols.

The first guerrilla attack occurred nine days after the war. Sabotage, mining, shooting, and mortaring incidents rapidly multiplied. The

A squad of Palestinian insurgents brief for an operation with the Jordan River as a backdrop. This was likely an event staged for the camera as they would cross at night and wear backpacks of food and equipment. Their principal firearm is the excellent Kalashnikov, but they would often carry a mix of weapons. (Albert Grandolini collection)

A scene played out many times over decades shows an IDF officer at a forward headquarters displaying to the press weapons captured from Palestinian guerrillas during recent action. Palestinian militant groups seeking to penetrate the occupied territories and Israel-proper to carry out acts of sabotage and terror were hunted and engaged by Zahal squads. Alternatively, the army crossed the river into Jordan in hot pursuit and pre-emptive actions, or air strikes reduced risk to Israeli personnel. (IDF)

Shelling and terror intrusions targeting civilian communities and infrastructure greatly angered the Israeli populace and government that was failing in its fundamental responsibility of providing security. Although such had been experienced since the founding of the state, the number of incidents increased and Israel's common disproportionate reprisals were swiftly meted out. Consequently, scenes like this Israeli housewife cleaning up after a shell hit her home was more often repeated in Arab lands and frequently from air attack. (IDF)

initial IDF responses were in August 1967 with shelling of bases inside refugee camps common. The first Israeli civilian fatality, a settler killed by a bomb, occurred on 1 October 1967. This allowed Israel to be tormented without jeopardising UAR national forces but disregarded any Jordanian displeasure.

Jordan's army also engaged is small arms exchanges and shelling – with or without authorisation – some as cover for Palestinian guerrillas or in response to Israeli reactions. The Jordanians, Iraqi troops stationed in Jordan, and Palestinian forces also shelled Israeli border settlements. The initial air action was on 21 November 1967 against Jordanian tanks. The first IAF loss on the front was suffered that day during such actions, the pilot murdered by civilians upon parachuting to the ground. As the combat expanded, despite all the overflights and bombing, the RJAF did not confront Israeli air activity. The army learned to fight without air cover. King Hussein made an impassioned speech that he would contain the irregulars, but his prime minister (PM) refuted that soon after. Within two weeks the cross-border incursions resumed. The King called everywhere for help but to little avail.

The Israeli approach became one of 'if our people cannot live in peace and quiet, neither shall those across the fence. We must make life bearable for us but unbearable for them. Every provocation will be responded to in kind.' Resources began to flow to IDF elements in the area to carry out what was expected to be a sustained and arduous campaign.

PALESTINIAN INSURGENCY

Palestinian irregular warfare had always consisted in large measure of terrorism in attacking Israeli civilian targets to instil fear and dismay. Egypt, Syria, and Iraq had particularly assisted in arming and training these organisations, while others helped with financing. In the aftermath of the war the number of additional or resurgent Palestinian militant groups of varying persuasions proliferated, more than 17 by 1970 and perhaps 20 ultimately. Some of these were more leftist, more violent, promoted international versus local attacks, and so on. They only minimally or not at all coordinated their policies, tactics, and operations.

Faced with the popularity of the terrorists, their acts emblazoned excitedly in Arab newspapers, the PLO adopted a more aggressive posture. It took in Fatah in 1968 and, through various machinations, Arafat became PLO chairman on 4 February 1969. This sought to restore the organisation's credibility with donors and to begin consolidating the disparate guerrilla groups under unified leadership. Attempts to unite the factions, particularly by Arafat who sought a greater leadership role, was largely futile.

Urban attacks in the territories and well inside Israel were typically perpetrated by the PFLP. Although terrorism had been a constant presence since before independence, it now reached new levels of mayhem with 'peacetime' civilian casualties the highest of any time in Israel's history. The worse of it came in February and March 1968 with more than 30 significant attacks. There were a series of bombings in Tel Aviv and other large cities but most attacks consisted of rock throwing, knifings, shootings, and grenade attacks. Of the more notorious acts was a car bombing in Jerusalem during November 1968 that killed 10 while leaving 18 injured. There were a rash of grenade attacks in Jerusalem during one night in August 1968 and a crowd of Jewish pilgrims were injured in a grenade blast during October while visiting a shrine. The carnage continued into 1969 that included bombing of a market in Jerusalem on 12 February and another car bomb explosion in Tel Aviv on 30 June. Scores were killed and maimed each year.[14] Just about any adverse event in Israel was claimed by one or more Palestinian fighting group as its handiwork. This reached ridiculous levels, to include taking credit for the death of Premier Eshkol from a heart attack.

Table3: Major Palestinian Political/Military Groups, 1967–1973[13]

Organisation	Leaders	Founding Date	Principal Base	Peak Personnel Strength
al-Fatah, military arm Asifa	Yasser Arafat	1959	Jordan, Lebanon	11,000
Palestine Liberation Organization (PLO), nominally not military	Ahmed Shukairy, Yasser Arafat	1964	dispersed	
Palestine Liberation Army (PLA)	(Syrian military)	1964	Syria	3,000–3,500
Palestine Popular Liberation Organization (PPLO)	Muhammad Fayyad Ibrahim Khraysha	1964	Jordan, Syria	200
as-Saiqa, also Vanguard for the Popular Liberation War (VPLW)	(Syrian military)	1966	Syria	2,000–5,000
Palestinian Popular Struggle Front (PPSF)	Samir Aousma	1967	Jordan, Lebanon	2,000
Popular Front for the Liberation of Palestine (PFLP)	George Habash	August 1967	Syria	1,500
Popular Front for the Liberation of Palestine - General Command (PFLP-GC)	Syrian army officer Ahmed Jibril (Abu Jihad)	1968	Syria	700–900
Popular Liberation Force (PLF) or Yarmuk Brigade			Gaza Strip	
Popular Democratic Front for the Liberation of Palestine (PDLFP or just DFLP)	Nayef Hawatmeh	April 1969	Jordan, Lebanon	1,500
Arab Liberation Front (ALF)	Zeid Heidar	April 1969	Iraq	500–700
Black September Organization (BSO)	Salah Khalaf, Abu Daoud	September 1970	dispersed	60
Popular Revolutionary Front for the Liberation of Palestine (PRFLP)	Abu Shibad	February 1972	Lebanon	

Table 4: Terrorist Attacks Inside Israel, 1967–1973[15]

Year	Johnston Archive			Middle East Record		
	Attacks	Killed	Injured	Attacks	Killed	Injured
1967	0	16 (0)	0			
1968	8	55 (21)	221	45	19 (19)	138 (2)
1969	12	33 (14)	133	76	8	106
1970	5	74 (18)	63	17	5	56
1971	2	18 (5)	36			
1972	7	46 (41)	97			
1973	1	27 (0)	18			

Israel responded to the violence with military crackdowns. Border Guards and Shin Bet (acronym-derived name from Sherut Bitahon) internal security teams worked in the West Bank to undermine sanctuary, recruitment, and subversive activities. During the investigations the security forces typically rounded up hundreds of Israeli Arabs and Palestinians in the territories. Expulsions and home demolition of those that collaborated with and harboured the insurgents soon undermined that source of support. In September 1967 alone the Israelis captured approximately 100 of the enemy. These operations greatly limited the growth and movement of the militants in the territory though cells of saboteurs continued to be uncovered and eliminated. From 1969 the attacks tapered off and by 1971 the subversive activity had dropped to almost nothing.

SPECIAL FORCES

As the War of Attrition heated up, Egypt and Israel conducted more and more special forces operations to an extent beyond anything they had undertaken to that time. Small force retaliatory strikes, day and night, had been a common feature of IDF operations, executing reprisal raids, while the Arabs had still to mature their teams.

The Egyptian specops units doubled in number to perhaps 20 during this period with ranger reconnaissance, airborne, and frogmen special forces while adapting to Mi-8 helicopters for airborne movement.[16] The paratroopers and as-Saiqa (Thunderbolt) commandos joined in a joint command during early 1969. The naval commando force was some 100 men strong. Attempts to employ Palestinian Liberation Army guerrillas into the specops on the canal was unsuccessful.

Syria had a modest commando force with a parachute battalion and Special Units (Wihdat Khasa), the latter expanded to five battalions, all under a special forces headquarters. The principal responsibility of these outfits was protecting the regime though they did execute some minor raids against IDF dispositions along the ceasefire line. It also encompassed one or two battalions of Palestinian units. Among the Palestinian units integrated into the Syrian Army was a Baathist-inspired as-Saiqa commando element that was directed in attacks inside Israel. Iraq sponsored its own unit as the Arab Liberation Force. Like their Syrian counterparts, the two Jordanian commando battalions and the Royal Guards focussed principally on protecting the monarchy but emphasising counter-insurgency, held in reserve to answer any threat from fedayeen.

The IDF had a number of reconnaissance units called sayeret (literally 'scout'), but they were all small outfits. Each territorial command created their own sayarot (plural) for reconnaissance and short-range raids in support of counter-insurgency operations. The most active sayerot were the paratrooper (Tzananhim) and navy commandos (Flotilla 13). The former had come to focus on heliborne operations. The most secretive operations were typically executed by sayeret Matkal (Unit 269) reporting directly to the chief-of-staff. Given the marginal combat capability of the Israel Navy, the service had always emphasised the role of its specops unit to penetrate enemy defences and engage enemy ships. The marine raiders of Flotilla 13 were equipped with explosive boats, rubber dinghies, kayaks, and small two-man submersible boats. The dismal performance the team during the Six-Day War meant the unit had to be rehabilitated and so they started small, worked with sayeret Matkal, and built to significant operations on their own. Initially the navy men operated the boats crossing any water barrier, no matter how small. This was intended to improve the naval personnel spirit and skills while gaining the trust of the General Staff. Soon the pace of operations made this impractical. The soldiers learned to cross water barriers while the sailors gained in ground combat capabilities. Flotilla 13 operations soon came to include the salvage divers of Unit 707 who operated the craft landing IDF teams and the held the beachhead until extraction.

All the conflict nations fielded paratroopers but none jumped into combat. Highly trained and well-equipped, they were elite units, especially the Israeli scout company of paratroopers, which were employed when a mission demanded their skills. These IDF paratroopers are seen preparing for a jump from a Noratlas transport. (Albert Grandolini collection)

The combatant navies and air forces contributed by transporting commandos or performing specops with their own teams, usually at night. The Israelis were generally more daring, executing larger and more complex raids than the Egyptians. As the irregular warfare grew, all teams contributed more and had to grow in size – though the IDF units were still composed of dozens of men (aside from paratroopers) while the Arab forces had hundreds. The Arabs saw only modest action while Zahal units were stressed by the high operations tempo yet competed for the most 'glamourous' missions.

5

AIR FORCES IN PLAY

The Israel Air Force had played a pivotal role in the Six-Day War and was expected to be vital during the combat challenges that lay ahead. However, it needed to reequip and constantly adjust to the new threats posed by weapons delivered to Israel's foes. The Arab states worked to assimilate those aircraft and air defence assets while waging a low-level war of increasing intensity. Some of the latest air combat systems in the world were brought into play with new tactics tested in battle.

OPPOSING AIR ARMS

Although they supplied a significant force of aircraft and associated weapons, the Egyptian and Syrian air forces only slowly ramped-up their contribution to ongoing fighting. They continually felt constrained by their sponsor as in the past the Soviets did not supply their best equipment, at least initially. Spares were evidently deliberately delivered in limited quantities as a form of restraint. This included such things as drop tanks without which operations were kept close to home bases. Egyptian industry began to produce high-usage spares and munitions to include the tanks. The Syrian air force remained comparatively inactive until fall 1972 even in the face of Israeli airstrikes in their territory. The Jordanians moved their aircraft far to the east and to Syria. These included their aging Hunters but also the Lockheed F-104s that began arriving from the USA in summer 1969 after being embargoed from before the war. They were forbidden to fly west of Amman. Aircraft and pilots were costly, and the RJAF did not risk them against a greatly superior foe, though their value was thus rendered almost moot. The Iraqis moved some aircraft to bases near the Jordanian border and based some in Syria but conducted no combat operations despite professed eagerness for battle.

Arab requests for more potent weapons and advanced aircraft, approaching the capabilities of the American systems being deliver to the Israelis, continued to meet with resistance. These included improved versions of the R-3 AAM and the new MiG-23 and Su-20 (export version of the Su-17M) fighter-bombers that could reach Israeli heartland airfields with some ordnance and advanced bombing avionics. The Soviets pointed out that their clients had yet to master the systems they had and were not ready to take on more. Fuming at the condescending attitude, the Arabs were sure that their supplier was intentionally limiting them to keep them dependent on the generosity of the Soviet Union, to avoid seeing their weapons cast in a bad light, and to prevent another war with potential confrontation with the West that might put in jeopardy the basing rights they enjoyed. Additionally, the Israelis had repeatedly obtained examples of weapons provided to the Arabs and the insights gained were expected to have been shared with the West in exchange for materiel. Further such leaks could jeopardise the success of any armed contest with NATO.

The lesser systems, comparatively quick training, low operating hours, and modest operational experience continued to place the Arab combatants at a disadvantage. Despite any martial ardour, they did not exploit the advantages they did enjoy with the boldness, determination, and devotion the Israelis displayed. The Arabs continued to be hamstrung with less intelligence on their adversary owing to comparatively deficient PR systems, electronic warfare (EW) capabilities, and human intelligence. There was also the battlefield in the home fronts with spying, subversive activity, and espionage by national intelligence services as well as the terrorists. The Egyptian command echelons, and those of other countries, were penetrated by Israeli agents and such achieved some noteworthy success. The Soviets may have been leery of sharing all they knew for fear of revealing intelligence collection means via leaks. When the USSR sent two fighter regiments to Egypt in early 1970 (see Volume 2, Chapter 5) the Israelis soon had a complete list of the pilots' names. The IDF also operated a Russian-language radio show from Sinai for the benefit of the USSR servicemen and family members inside Egypt. Even Israelis were recruited by foreign intelligence collection organisations.

Although these air forces were reequipped within months, and eventually to higher levels than prior to the war, they were by no means fit to take on even the reduced IAF much less that which grew in a few years. General Fawzi assessed that the UARAF reached quantitative par with the IAF six months after the war, but 2.5 years to reach operational par.[1] Much rehabilitation and retraining were

As an indication of stretching every shekel, the IAF continued to operate Second World War surplus C-47 Dakota transports for general transport and low-stress special roles like communications relay. Many personnel flew between Israel-proper and posts in Sinai aboard the spartan airplanes, such as this aircraft at Lod from 122 Squadron formed in 1971. (Author's collection)

CAPTURED ENEMY AIR COMBAT SYSTEMS

The Israelis had some close insight into opposition airplanes, missiles, and other systems via several means. An Iraqi pilot was induced to defect to Israel with a MiG-21F-13 in 1966. The jet was extensively tested and combat trials taught the best manner in which to defeat the MiG-21. Two MiG-17Fs came in 1968 via a pair of Syrian student pilots who accidentally landed at an Israeli dispersal field in the far north of the country. Numbered 1033 and 1041, they had been flown by Walid Adham Ibrahim al-Wallid and Ridwan Radfan Rifai. These, too, were evaluated and flown in training with IAF interceptors. The S-75 SAMs overrun in Sinai, albeit damaged, plus captured R-3S AAMs and P-10 radar, also provided insight. The P-12 radar snatched in December 1969 (see Volume 2, Chapter 3) was another boon. Rumours of other combat aircraft captured by Israel during the period have not been substantiated.[2] Arab forces were evidently less diligent in examining wrecks but did recover unexploded missiles and other hardware, likely all shared with the USSR.

The Israeli's 'captive' MiG-21F-13 seen in 1968 with the added red markings signifying a 'friendly' and the amusing 007 nose markings suggesting the secret agent James Bond. The aircraft came via an Iraqi defector in 1966 and was employed in mock air combat to teach IAF interceptor pilots the best means to defeat the jet. The year 1968 is likely the last in which it was operated in Israel. (Ra'anan Weiss collection)

Two Syrian MiG-17s were mistakenly landed at the far north dispersal airfield of Bezet on 12 August 1968. These were operated by the IAF in dissimilar air combat manoeuvring exercises. Here one of these aircraft is seen on display for visitors with the Syrian markings painted out and red/white colours added to aid identification as a 'friendly.' (Albert Grandolini collection)

At least one of the MiG-17s and the MiG-21 were provided to the USA during 1968 and 1969 for evaluation. The same was done with many other captured weapons, intelligence information, and combat lessons. The Israelis tended to withhold such prizes until they could be swapped for guarantees of American equipment deliveries. This became a long-running quid pro quo between the two nations' militaries but was rare before 1969 as Israel was attempting to maintain good relations with the USSR in deference to Jews seeking to emigrate to Israel. Soviet combat personnel deployments to Egypt ended such restraint. Rumours of captured aircraft used by the IAF in clandestine operations are almost certainly false.[3]

performed, drawing upon the lessons of the war and as guided by Soviet advisors who repeatedly urged restraint and sometimes succeeded in altering operational plans. This built resentment, both at the control by foreigners and the perceived lack of aggressiveness by the political echelon. It caused friction that, at one point, resulted in a four-day sit-down strike by the UARAF.[4]

Many air arms were interested in the IAF's experience meeting Soviet systems in combat. Yet, the air force remained an enigma to most outsiders as Israelis were exceptionally security-conscious and gave few insights into the workings of its Ministry of Defence (MoD). They felt a collective sense of isolation and holding against outside threats given the continuing military conflict and guarded support from distant friendly nations. Unit identifications and locations were suppressed, and personnel kept anonymous. Air bases were not marked on maps and were screened by stands of eucalyptus trees. Aircraft markings were obliterated from photographs or covered during public displays, or a third digit added to exposed two-digit serials. Even when dealing officially with friendly nations Israel aggressively sought assets and information it desired while giving little in return or delivered grudgingly. The Arab countries were even more guarded and few foreigners had the ability to gain any insight.

With the Israelis struggling to pay for a first-class force and the Arabs constrained by the Soviets, it was a 'poor man's' fight compared to Korea and Vietnam, or even the Indo-Pakistani war of 1965. Innovation was the order of the day. However, the War of Attrition showed off the air weapons of East versus West in unprecedented fashion.

Table 5 shows the state of the depleted Arab confrontation states' air forces immediately following the war compared with that of Israel. Of course, the Arab forces were staggering from their defeat and would have been challenged to conduct major offensive combat operations as they began undertaking significant reformation. Yet, the IAF had lost significant number of combat aircraft, with others in repair, and munitions were depleted. It could not have repeated its 5 June attacks.

Table 5: Air Combat Systems 11 June 1967

System	Egypt	Syria	Jordan	Israel	System
Fighter-Bomber					
MiG-21	22	35	-	61	Mirage III
MiG-19	11	-	-	21	Super Mystère
MiG-17	26	28	-	26	Mystère IVA
MiG-15	11	-	-	41	Ouragan
Su-7	1	-	-	38	Magister
Hunter	-	-	4		
Bomber					
Tu-16	0	-	-	15	Vautour II
Il-28	0	2	-		
Assault Helicopters					
Mi-6	2	-	-	4	Super Frelon
Mi-8	-	-	-	28	S-58 & H-34
Combat Transports					
not employed tactically	-	-	-	22	Noratlas
Antiaircraft					
S-75 (launchers)	150	about 60 (not deployed)	-	6 batteries (5 deployed) 50 missiles*	Hawk
85mm	120	48	188 40mm	112 (34 batteries)	40mm
57mm	122	56		14 batteries	30mm
37mm	92	68	12 20mm	514 (5 batteries)	20mm
Some Arab numbers are best estimates or otherwise not reliably verified					
* Best estimate. Non-deployed batteries were likely in reserve					

Table 6 shows the IAF order-of-battle (ORBAT) immediately following the war, although not all aircraft were operational at any one time (typically 18–24 per squadron). Similar tables for the Arab confrontation states' forces would be misleading as many units had been effectively destroyed or rendered operationally irrelevant by combat losses and leadership purges.

Table 6: Israeli Air Combat ORBAT, 11 June 1967

Base	Unit	Aircraft	Notes
Wing 1			
Ramat David	107 Squadron	Ouragan	
	109 Squadron	Mystère IVA	
	110 Squadron	Vautour	8 IIA, 5 IIN, 2 IIB (modified to IIBR photo-recce)
	117 Squadron	Mirage *	
Wing 4			
Hatzor	101 Squadron	Mirage	
	105 Squadron	Super Mystère B2	
	113 Squadron	Ouragan	
Wing 6			
Hatzerim	147 Squadron (reserve)	Magister	lightly armed, seconded from training
Wing 8			
Tel Nof	103 Squadron	Noratlas	
	114 Squadron	Super Frelon	
	116 Squadron	Mystère IVA	
	119 Squadron	Mirage	
	124 Squadron	S-58 & H-34	
* Mirages included 56 IIICJ, 3 IIIBJ twin-seat, and 2 Mirage IIICJ(R) photo-recce assets, all combat-capable			

EGYPT

The UARAF was the darling of Egypt's military services and the pride of Nasser. Consequently, their defeat within hours on 5 June was a severe blow to the state and the morale of its personnel. Thirty-three combat pilots had been killed, or around 14 percent of the cadre. Others were imprisoned or banned from flying because of questionable loyalty.[5] Consequently, there was much rebuilding and rehabilitation to perform.

Egypt's air force reflected the same sharp division between officers and enlisted personnel as the rest of the military. Many of the officers possessed a modest sense of duty and commitment to hard work. Consequently, rehabilitation did not just focus on reequipping the force but also changing the service's culture to truly seek proficiency, fighting spirit and devotion to the state. Hundreds of new ground and air personnel were required, trained to the point of combat introduction. For many this included basic education to work with sophisticated military hardware. An air force high school was established as a path to the academy and an air defence college stood up. Given the government's stated goal of a rematch with Israel within a year or two, all reformation had to be performed at a rapid pace. All these factors continued to undermined readiness and combat capabilities.

Egypt was given priority in the Soviet arms shipments in June 1967 and aircraft were the first to come via the mammoth airlift. By the end of 1967 the UARAF had 105 percent of its pre-war strength, counting airframes alone.

Nasser sought to more than double the size of the UARAF from 260 combat aircraft to 600. Despite the UARAF's growth during this period personnel remained steady at 15,000. The plan included having two bases for each squadron such the unit would not be reduced to total ineffectiveness by one being rendered inoperative. Over the next few years Egypt built 15 new bases and dispersal fields with a minimum two runways plus taxiways that could be used for take-off and landing. Existing fields were expanded similarly. Five highway stretches were also reinforced to be employed for flight operations and included nearby HAS. Fields near the front served as emergency recovery strips for aircraft at critical fuel states following combat. The construction programme also included about 1,000 concrete-covered revetments and some 500 HAS at 20 combat airbases. New buildings for all purposes were usually built underground. These encompassed command centres, operations rooms, maintenance shops, and the like. This was an immense effort consuming thousands of tonnes of concrete and employing tens of thousands of labourers. Just through the end of 1967 Egypt spent $315 million on such construction projects.

Air defences around the bases were beefed-up. Runway damage repair teams were increased in number and given additional training and equipment. The surveillance radar network of 47 or more stations had used old equipment and was not integrated with intercept control. The network was expanded with gear more suited to detect aircraft in the combat area flying below 500m (1,500ft). These included a large station atop Mount Ataka near Suez. Coverage was still lacking for the area east of the mountains along the Gulf of Suez and the IAF exploit this to infiltrate. Egypt also established radar stations in Jordan, manned by Egyptian personnel, to better monitor IAF traffic en route to the Suez front.

Table 7: Egyptian Air Combat ORBAT, 1969–1972

Base	Unit	Aircraft	Notes
Air Brigade 102 (assigned to Air Defence Command)			
Inchas	No. 25 Squadron	MiG-21PFS	
	No. 26 Squadron	MiG-21F-13	
	No. 27 Squadron	MiG-21MF	established March 1970
Air Brigade 104 (previously Air Brigade 233, assigned to Air Defence Command)			
el-Mansourah then Ghardaka	No. 45 Squadron	MiG-21PFS	
	No. 47 Squadron	MiG-21PFM	
Air Brigade 111			
Ghardaka	No. 43 Squadron	MiG-21FL, MiG-21PFM	established 1970 with assets from No. 47 Squadron
	No. 44 Squadron	MiG-21PFS	
Air Brigade 201			
Qwaysina and Ghardaka	No. 15 Squadron	MiG-17F	
Qwaysina	No. 25 Squadron	MiG-17F	
Air Brigade 203 (308 from mid-1969)			
Bilbeis	No. 87 Squadron	Su-7BMK	
	No. 89 Squadron	Su-7BMK	
Air Brigade 205 (305 from mid-1969)			
el-Mansourah and Abu Hammad and Qwaysina	No. 52 Squadron	MiG-17F	later No. 71 Squadron
Ras Banas and Ghardaka and el-Mansourah	No. 53 Squadron	MiG-17F	later No. 86 Squadron
Air Brigade 306 (established late 1969)			
Ghardaka	No. 61 Squadron	MiG-17F	established 1970 or 1971
Almaza and al-Fayyum and Daraw and el-Mansourah	No. 89 ? Squadron	MiG-17F	
Air Brigade 403 (established 1970 or 1971)			
Aswan	No. 34 Squadron	Tu-16	re-established September 1967, 9 aircraft, later No. 75 Squadron
	No. 36 Squadron	Tu-16K-11-16	re-established November 1971, later No. 76 Squadron
Air Brigade 407 (established 1970 or 1971)			

Egypt's Army worked hard to obtain improved armoured personnel carriers and some of these were to be amphibious as the army began training for a canal crossing operation. These included some Soviet BTR-50s and many hundreds of Czech OT-62s derived from the Soviet vehicle. Many of the East European armoured vehicles suffered from the heat and sand of the Middle East, with crew likewise suffering from poor ventilation and interior cooling. (Artwork by David Bocquelet)

Thanks to deliveries from the USSR, which began arriving in September–October 1967, the Egyptian Army moved quickly after the war to replace outdated equipment including Second World War vintage armoured vehicles. They greatly increased the number of T-54/55 tanks with the generous assistance of the USSR. This T-54 carries a heavy machine gun on the turret roof that could be effective against low-flying aircraft. (Artwork by David Bocquelet)

The thin-skinned and open-top BTR-152 armoured personnel carrier was still heavily used during the late 1960s and shown here is a Syrian example, which had wide stripes in yellow sand over its original green overall colour. Both the Egyptians and Syrians sought a halftrack or a fully tracked armoured personnel carrier, like the US-made M3s and, later on, M113s operated by the Israelis – for better performance on sand and with an enclosed fighting compartment – but the Soviets and their allies had little of that kind to offer at the time. (Artwork by David Bocquelet)

Israel operated a small number of Panhard AML-90 armoured cars, with a 90mm gun, only briefly following the war. They were considered too vulnerable even for urban combat as recoilless rifles, bazookas and rocket-propelled grenades made their way into the Palestinian militants' arsenals. Smoke grenade launch tubes have been affixed to the aft portion of the turret in this example. (Artwork by David Bocquelet)

The Israeli Army operated a vast number of Second World War vintage vehicles and guns. Many had been modernised as budgets permitted including the Sherman tank. The M-50 Super Sherman had a French 75mm gun that required a counterweight to be added to the rear of the turret. A diesel engine, upgraded suspension and wide tracks were additional features. The tank was employed to good effect in the Six-Day War and persisted after. (Artwork by David Bocquelet)

The British Centurion, with its 105mm gun, was the most advanced tank employed by the IDF during the war. The Israelis were keen to replace the gasoline engine with a diesel for combat survivability and to improve the transmission. This upgrade program was ongoing throughout the inter-war years, the example shown here with the revised engine deck coming with the diesel. The American .30cal machine gun at the commander's hatch was ubiquitous on most IDF armoured vehicles. (Artwork by David Bocquelet)

The Israel Air Force only slowly transitioned from French warplanes to American during this period, owing mostly to budget and measured exports into the region by the USA. Consequently, the notably antiquated Dassault Ouragan continued to be operated by a single unit (113 Squadron, badge shown in tail) into 1973. This example carries unguided 127mm rockets, which were still effective against some bunkers, vehicles and buildings. (Artwork by Luca Canossa)

Another ageing French type operated by the IAF was the Dassault Mystère IVA, seen here in the three-tone upper surface scheme adopted during this period. It carries the 116 Squadron tail badge, a 250kg bomb under each wing, and two external tanks. The 'kill' roundel on the nose was repeated on many Israeli fighters after the Six-Day War and more collected during the War of Attrition. The 'campaign ribbons' on the tail are for the 1956 Sinai Campaign and the Six-Day War. (Artwork by Tom Cooper)

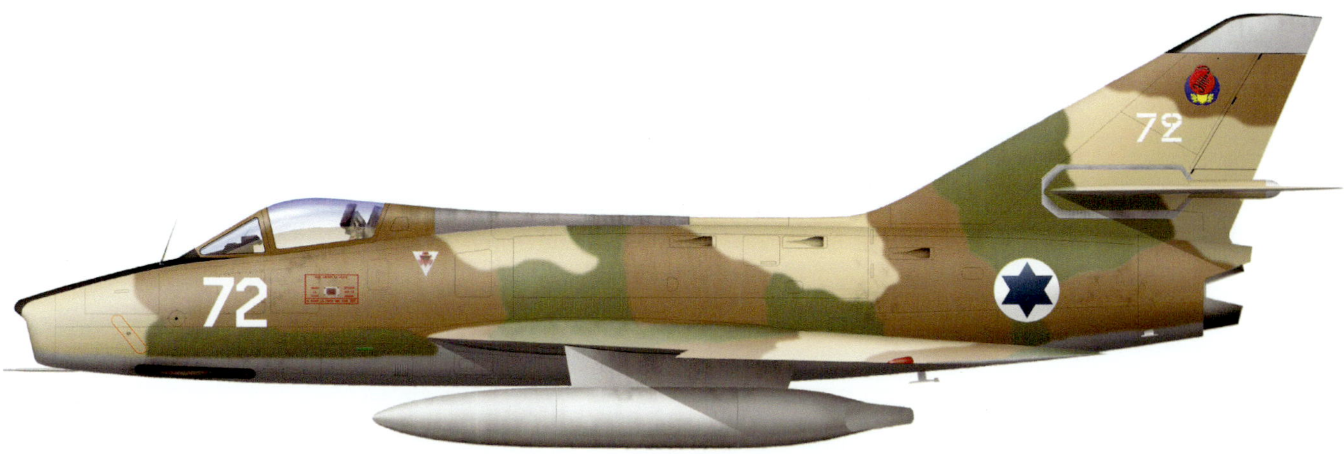

A single squadron of the IAF (No. 105, badge on tail) operated Dassault Super Mystère B.2 fighter-bombers, employed exclusively in ground attack. The drag chute house on the trailing edge of the vertical tail, in line with the horizontal, became endemic to all Israeli fighters – and was added to the new A-4H Skyhawks – as they prepared to land on cratered runways in the event the Arab air forces inflicted a similar debilitating airfield strike campaign on IAF bases as that service had delivered to the Arabs on 5 June 1967. (Artwork by Tom Cooper)

Mirage IIICJs were the principle Israeli interceptor throughout the War of Attrition, forsaking ground attack as the new Skyhawks came to dominate that role. Air-to-air missiles remained in short supply owing to cost and slow production of the locally developed Shafrir. Consequently, the three Mirage squadrons adopted Soviet R-3S missiles from UARAF stock captured at the abandoned Bir Gifgafa AB. They still frequently flew with just one AAM. This 119 Squadron jet carries one of these rounds under the port wing and shows the natural metal finish of the early post-war period with 119 Squadron tail flash and two kills (Egyptian and Jordanian). (Artwork by Tom Cooper)

Often counted as one of the 'hostile Arab nations surrounding little Israel', Lebanon was smaller in all respects and with no aggressive intentions towards its southern neighbour. However, in a 'rough neighbourhood', it made a modest effort at arming its small armed forces with some effective weapons. Among these was a single squadron of Dassault Mirage IIIEL fighters, the acquisition of which was financed by the Arab League but discontinued because of the rampant corruption of the irresponsible Lebanese officers. Lebanese Mirages were never flown in action against Israel: instead, in 1970 they flew a few air strikes on Palestinians in the south of the country, usually in the configuration shown here, armed with combined external fuel tank and rocket launchers for 68mm unguided rockets. (Artwork by Tom Cooper)

The Royal Jordanian Air Force had long relied on the excellent Hawker Hunter fighter-bomber. Its pre-war fleet was destroyed in June 1967, but replaced by new acquisitions from a variety of sources immediately after: two years later, No. 1 Squadron was completely restored on Hunter F.Mk 73As (equivalent of the FAB.Mk 9). Unlike earlier times, and while flying attack missions during the internal unrest in 1970, they avoided contact with the IAF. (Artwork by Tom Cooper)

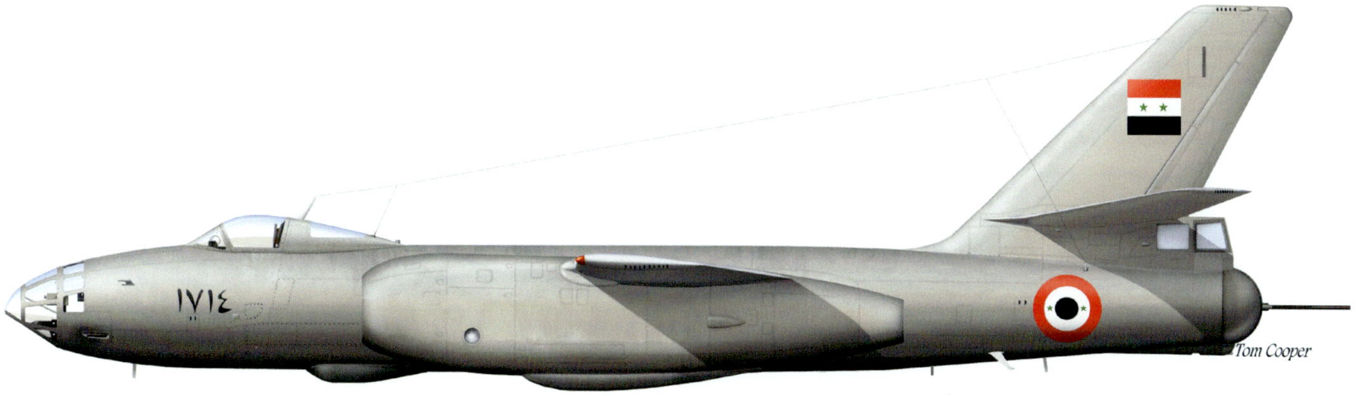

The Il-28 jet bomber was so aged by the June 1967 War, especially in the face of demonstrably effective Israeli air defences, that flying it into combat was a very worrying proposition. Losses were replaced by 10 aircraft acquired from the USSR and 12 from Algeria: these were primarily employed for maritime patrol duties. This illustration shows aircraft serial number 1714, still in 'silver grey' overall (two layers of clear lacquer, mixed with 10 percent and 5 percent aluminium powder, respectively), still common for most of 1967. (Artwork by Tom Cooper)

This Egyptian MiG-21F-13 was one of 22 aircraft of this type that survived the June 1967 Arab-Israeli War, and was camouflaged using car paints immediately after. These were applied 'around' its black identification stripes on the rear fuselage and wingtips. It is shown armed with its standard complement of two R-3S air-to-air missiles (one under each wing). The low reliability of this weapon meant that the MiG-21F-13s internal 30mm cannon were much treasured and ensured the model continued to operate beside later models in which the guns had been deleted. Notably, the 'expendable' drop tank was commonly left unpainted, but the jet's serial number (5341) was repeated on it in black. (Artwork by Tom Cooper)

The Sukhoi Su-7BMK became the principal attack jet of the Arab air forces in the years following the June 1967 Arab-Israeli War – although its range and payload were significantly less than Western types. This Egyptian example, serial 7340, is shown as armed with an OFAB-250-230 high-explosive/incendiary bomb: a weapon added to the arsenal of this type only after its delivery to Egypt. In similar fashion, it was the Egyptians that began adding rear-view mirrors to the cockpit transparencies of their Su-7BMKs in 1967. Over the following two years, they added the second hardpoint under each wing, thus greatly increasing the total warload the jet could carry. All of these modifications were eventually adopted by the Soviets and their allies in Europe, the Middle East, and in India. (Artwork by Tom Cooper)

Of the few remaining Vautour bombers in 110 Squadron the IAF had two of the IIB variant in which the 'glass' nose allowed for a camera mount in addition to a camera package that could be carried in the weapons bay. Aircraft 33 was nicknamed 'Big Brother' (applied in Hebrew, in red, with black 'shadows', low on the left side of the nose), and is shown as it appeared during 1970, equipped with external tanks and two Shafrir air-to-air missiles for self-defence. Only one of these aircraft remained after its twin was shot down on 1 December 1967 by Egyptian AAA. (Artwork by Tom Cooper)

The IDF greatly valued aerial photo-reconnaissance and its two Mirage IIIRJ aircraft were heavily tasked with flying penetrations deep over neighbouring countries. This example – serial (7)89 (the other was (7)99) – is shown with a Tarmil nose for vertical photography, though this could be swapped with noses containing alternative camera arrangements. It displayed the badge of No. 119 Squadron on the fin, and the colour scheme adopted in 1969. (Artwork by Tom Cooper)

The Egyptians were just as adamant as the Israelis about the importance of aerial reconnaissance but lacked the resources Israel was able to bring to bear as the USSR was reluctant to supply suitable aircraft and cameras. Consequently, UARAF workshops developed their own gear, including a modified 490-litre centreline tank for a MiG-21, with a dry bay for a British-made Vinten F40 camera, as shown in the left lower corner of this artwork. The jet – a MiG-21FL serial number 5260 – was another survivor of the June 1967 Arab-Israeli War and is known to have carried R-3S missiles for self-defence. (Artwork by Tom Cooper)

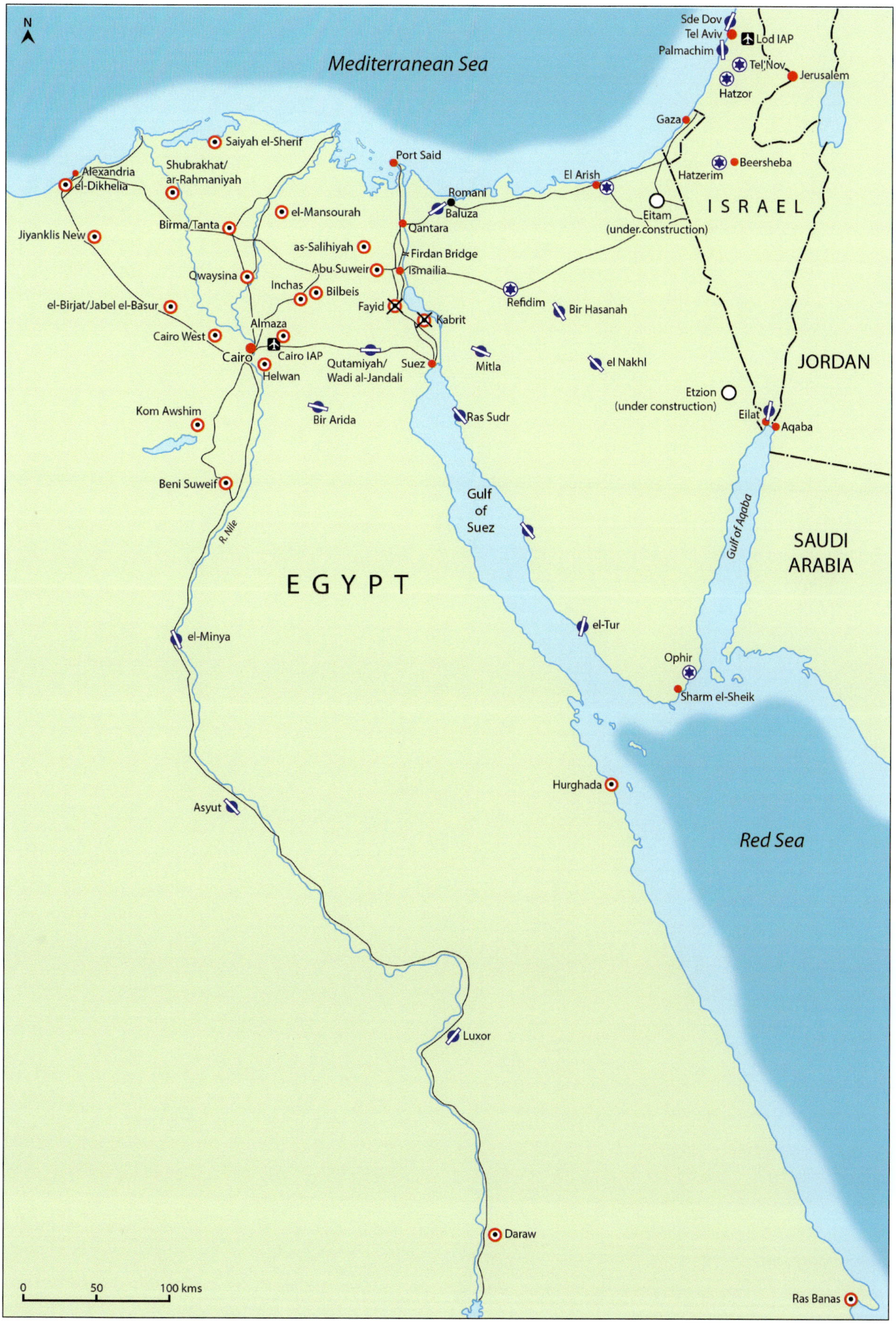

The Egyptian and Israeli airbases in the Suez Canal warzone are shown in about 1972. There were more dispersal and recovery strips not depicted, and Israel had airstrips in Sinai for light airplanes to operate near remote installations. The growth in number of UARAF bases is realised by comparison to the map in Chapter 1. The IAF could reach most of the Egyptian bases shown with their F-4Es (arriving fall 1969) and all in the Nile Delta with their other fighter-bombers even flying from Israel-proper. The UARAF could barely reach el Arish with their bombers and even assets beyond the Sinai western plain could not be touched with any respectable ordnance load by existing fighter-bombers. (Map by George Anderson)

The northern and eastern front air bases encompassed Israel, Jordan, Syria, and Lebanon. The range of IAF fighter-bombers placed western Jordanian and southern Syrian bases within easy reach if Israel chose to execute strikes on these installations. Reaching Israeli bases with Soviet-built fighter-bombers with any respectable weapon load was more problematic. (Map by George Anderson)

Cairo West	No. 8 Squadron	Il-28	later No. 75 Squadron
	No. 9 Squadron	Il-28	later No. 76 Squadron
Air Brigade 515			
Almaza	No. 7 Squadron	Mi-8	
	No. 12 Squadron	Mi-8	
	No. 22 Squadron	Mi-8	
Air Brigade 533 (established 1970 or 1971, reconnaissance)			
Inchas	No. 5 Squadron	Su-7BMK	
Cairo West	No. 20 Squadron	Il-28R	
Inchas and as-Salihiyah	No. 21 Squadron	MiG-21RF	
Independent Units (reporting directly to UARAF Headquarters)			
Inchas	No. 46 Squadron	MiG-21F-13	reconnaissance, expanded in 1970 as Air Brigade 533
Tanta	No. 55 Squadron	Su-7BMK	
Alexandria, Mersa Matruh	No. 90 Reconnaissance Squadron (Soviet)	Tu-16R, Il-38, Be-12	deployed 1968, initially independent
Cairo West		Tu-16P, An-12PP	deployed 1970, 90th Independent Reconnaissance Aviation Squadron
106 Fighter Brigade (USSR 135th Fighter Aviation Regiment, deployed 1970)			
Beni Suweif	No. 60 Squadron	MiG-21SM	Soviet 1st Squadron
	No. 63 Squadron	MiG-21SM	Soviet 2nd Squadron
Kom Awshim	No. 65 Squadron	MiG-21SM	Soviet 3rd Squadron
108 Fighter Brigade (USSR 35th Independent Reconnaissance Aviation Squadrons, deployed 1970)			
Jiyanklis	No. 64 Squadron	MiG-21RF	Soviet 1st Flight
	No. 68 Squadron	MiG-21SM	Soviet 2nd Flight
	No. 70 Squadron	MiG-21SM	Soviet 3rd Flight
Cairo West	63rd Air Group	MiG-25RB (4 aircraft)	Soviet reconnaissance squadron, deployed March 1971–summer 1972
Date span for establishment of units indicates uncertainty. Squadrons typically carried 15–20 aircraft			

The S-75 batteries (specifically SA-75MK Dvina, NATO codename SA-2B 'Guideline' Mod 1) were fully deployed and supplemented with two replacements supplied by the Soviets for a total 27 and around 200 launchers. These were principally placed to defend eastern approaches to Cairo and the airbases in the area. Over two nights in perhaps spring 1968, 24 new sites were constructed in the eastern desert for positioning options. Antiaircraft artillery (AAA) consisted of 12 battalions with more than 1,000 guns, mostly visually directed. Given the importance of degrading the IAF in any future war, and the long road to building a fighter-intercept force capable of meeting the Israelis at some level of equivalent capabilities, Air Defence Command (ADC) was created on 1 February 1968 as a separate and equal service. General Ali Mustafa el-Baghdadi initially commanded, relieved in May 1969 by Major General Mohammed Ali Fahmy. Senior ADC personnel were sent for courses in the USSR.

Egypt was eventually divided into six air defence zones with separate control centres and assigned ground-control interception (GCI). Most active was that covering the canal area and so was given the best resources including seven S-75 batteries. Zones commanded air defence regiments (AAA, SAMs, and interceptors) defending high-value locations and ground combat units. Hence, the surveillance radar network and air force interceptors on air defence alert also fell under their direction. The principal combat control element was the brigade in which the ADC commander and an air force colonel worked together in identifying targets and countermeasures, then launching interceptors or directing a missile battalion to engage.

Table 8: Air Defence Command, February 1969–January 1970

Zone	Headquarters	Sector/Remarks
2 – East	al-Firdan	Suez Canal
3 – Central	Cairo, al-Zamalik	Cairo
4 – North	Alexandria	coastal
5 – South	Aswan	Upper Egypt, also training
6 – Nile Delta	el-Mansourah AB	central Nile Delta

In 1972, Saudi Arabia promised 20 Lightning fighters excess to need. The UARAF sent seven pilot and 33 mechanics for training. With poor serviceability of the aircraft and lacklustre instruction, the team returned after nearly a year emptyhanded. A Kuwaiti squadron of Lightnings did deploy to Egypt. Egyptian aircrew were also sent to Libya, Kuwait, and elsewhere to train on aircraft that might come Egypt's way during a war.

Those observing UARAF operations usually came away unimpressed. Aircraft in-service rates were approximately 50–60 percent. Egypt committed their air force much less than did Israel. The IDF observed UARAF flights hastily striking a target and then hurrying away without ensuring it was destroyed – although some of this was surely due to short endurance of the jets. In some cases the ordnance was expended far from the target in order to avoid being engaged by defences. Beginning in July 1969 the UARAF began to include suppression of enemy air defences (SEAD) in their attacks.

A Saudi Arabian Lightning performs a loop while carrying a Red Top AAM. A potent fighter jet, the Saudis promised to lend a squadron of their Lightnings to the UARAF and Egyptian personnel began the requisite training. However, like many other such offers after the Six-Day War, this did not pan out owing to poor serviceability of the aircraft and mediocre training. (Albert Grandolini collection)

Table 9: Syrian Air Combat ORBAT, 1968–1970

Base	Unit	Aircraft	Notes
		Air Brigade 3	
T-4	No. 9 Squadron	MiG-21F-13	added MiG-21RF from 1970, MiG-21MF from 1971
Tsaykel	No. 11 Squadron	MiG-21PFM	established 1970 through 1972
Dmeyr	No. 67 Squadron	MiG-21FL, MiG-21PFM	
		Air Brigade ?	
Abu ad-Duhor	No. 8 Squadron	MiG-21PFM	MiG-21PFM from 1970 or 1971
Hamah	No. 10 Squadron	MiG-21PFM	established 1970 or 1971
Dhab'ah	No. 12 Squadron	MiG-21PFM	established 1970 or 1971
		Air Brigade 7	
Almazza	No. 5 Squadron	MiG-17F	
Khalkalah	No. 7 Squadron	MiG-17F	established 1970
Almazza	No. 15 Squadron	MiG-17F	with UARAF No. 62 Squadron from 1972
		Air Brigade 17	
Nasiriyeh	No. 54 Squadron	MiG-17F	
Bley	No. 68 Squadron	MiG-17F	established 1969 through 1971
Tha'leh	No. 77 Squadron	MiG-17F	established 1970 or 1971
		Air Brigade ?	
Dmeyr	No. 19 Squadron	Su-7MK	established 1968 or 1969
Sh'eirat	No. 27 Squadron	Su-7MK	established 1968 or 1969
		Air Brigade ?	
Marj as-Sultan	No. 25 Squadron	Mi-8	
	No. 32 Squadron	Mi-8	
	No. 37 Squadron	Mi-8	
Date span for establishment of units indicates uncertainty. Squadrons were typically 12–16 aircraft			

SYRIA

Expansion of the Syrian Arab Air Force to a level capable of engaging the Israelis successfully was slow. The USSR gave priority to Egypt and were less than enamoured with Syrian leadership. In late 1967 and early 1968 aircraft deliveries included 20 MiG-21PFMs, 10 MiG-17F and Polish Lim-5 equivalent, 12 Su-7BMKs, and 22 Mi-8s. The USSR finally consented to additional deliveries in late 1969 and into 1970. These included 20 or more MiG-17s, 16 MiG-21MFs, and six MiG-21RF photo-reconnaissance platforms. The SyAAF was also enforced by visiting UARAF squadrons throughout the period. The radar network was slow to be upgraded and the Israelis exploited the weakness.

The August 1968 mistaken landing of two MiG-17Fs in Israel provided the excuse for General Assad to purge high ranking officers and shuffle leadership. This was so disruptive that a dozen pilots defected to Iraq and nearly 200 other personnel fled, further delaying rehabilitation of the force.

JORDAN

The restoration of the RJAF was also slow, both for economic and equipment delivery reasons plus lack of urgency. It gradually acquired replacement Hawker Hunters, long its principal fighter-bomber. These included four from the UK, five from Saudi Arabia in early 1968, and 10 from Lebanon in 1969. Grants from oil-rich Arab nations allowed 15 reconditioned Hunters to be acquired from Hawker Siddeley, delivered by 1969. The Hunter units were thus an amalgamation of various models. The assets were moved to distant bases in the east because western airfields were being repaired and the IAF threat was overwhelming.

Table 10: Jordan Air Combat ORBAT, 1967–1971

Base	Unit	Aircraft	Notes
Mafraq	No. 1 Squadron	5 Hunter F.Mk 73A	in Syria 1967–1969
	No. 6 Squadron	19 Hunter FGA.Mk 9	from 1971
H-5	No. 9 Squadron	22 F-104A, 4 TF-104B*	from mid-1969

The reconditioned aircraft equivalent to FGA.Mk 9s were termed F.Mk 73As. Even the FGA.Mk 9s of No. 6 squadron were a collection of aircraft originally of other models.
* Nine F-104As were lent to Pakistan in December 1971 during the Indo-Pakistan war and one was shot down there in combat.

LEBANON

During the war the Lebanese Air Force (Force Aérienne Libanaise, FAL) had attempted to prevent IAF aircraft from violating Lebanon airspace and lost a Hunter for its troubles. They never again challenged Israeli intrusions that became frequent. They could contribute only modestly to internal armed struggles. While some funding from other Arab states assisted the FAL growing following the war, this was minor owing to these factors and fiscal impediments.

The Soviets delivered Mi-8 assault helicopters to its Arab allies following the war. This Egyptian example carries rocket pods, but the type became the common mount for airborne special operations units, especially at night. (via Group 73)

The aging Hunter still had some manoeuvring advantages over Israeli jets but was heavily outnumbered and deficient in most other aspects of air combat. Against ground targets it could still perform respectably. Consequently, given budget limitations, the RJAF gathered more Hunters and steered clear of the IAF. (Albert Grandolini collection)

Jordan waited a long time for their Starfighters after the USA embargoed delivery before the June 1967 war. They were delivered reluctantly given growing American accommodation to Israel. Some in the American public would have preferred some means of ensuring that these F-104s could never assume a westerly heading and so potentially threaten Israel. (Albert Grandolini collection)

In the late 1960s the combat means of the FAL was made up of two fighter squadrons with 19 Hunters and 10 Mirage IIIELs. The Mirages came with Matra R.530 AAM but were otherwise poorly equipped. Seldom flown and then stored, they were eventually sold to Pakistan and Hunters to Jordan. Five lightly armed Fouga Magister trainers were also available, increased to 11 in 1972. Air defence was made up of fixed and mobile guns of light calibre. A very capable French early warning radar was installed on Jebel Barouk. Air bases were Beirut IAP (Khalde), Rayak and Kleyate.

PALESTINE

The Palestinians established an embryonic air arm titled Force 14. Members were trained by Arab air forces and some of these had Palestinian units. Force 14 acquired some light airplanes of its own.

ISRAEL

The Israel Air Force consisted of approximately 9,000 career personnel, 1,000 conscripts, and around 10,000 reservists at any given time. There were approximately 375 combat aircrew including reservists and Emergency-Posting pilots.

The IAF lost 46 combat aircraft and 25 aircrew killed during the war. This represented 23 percent of fighter-bombers and 9 percent of combat pilots. For such a small force these were significant losses. Regardless, whatever rational operational scenario could be suggested the Israelis would still have emerged victorious given their severely depleted opposition. The IAF's initial focus was training to replace aircrew while damaged aircraft were refurbished – both requiring time. The operations tempo gradually increased to a level not seen before the war and so losses continued.

Acquiring warplanes, new or used, had always been difficult for Israel. Foreign powers had been leery of adding more into the volatile region and because of Israel's long-standing policy of disproportionate reprisals for cross-border guerrilla incidents. With the Arabs evidently willing to wield the 'oil sword' against the West, plus pressuring countries and companies to recognise the Arab Boycott, there were few nations disposed to sell arms to Israel.

The French embargo appeared to eliminate that source. President de Gaulle made the embargo complete following the Israeli raid on Beirut International Airport at the end of 1968 (see Volume 2, Chapter 1) during which French-supplied helicopters were employed. Israeli cargo transport flights to and from France to bring back vital supplies continued until just hours before the embargo became total. However, individual French ministries and industry quietly supported the weapons already delivered, in defiance of policy. Spares and ancillary equipment continued to flow, albeit at a diminishing rate, amounting to $175 million of value by 1971 alone. In some cases the Israelis were permitted to buy additional equipment on existing orders, but no new orders would be negotiated. Some gear was transhipped through third parties. After de Gaulle's resignation in April 1969 French industries appeared more open to the Israelis. The embargo was lifted in autumn 1973 but France avoided overt arms sales to Israel because of lucrative contacts with Arab trading partners.

The Israelis also took extraordinary measures to continue operating their French equipment. Proficiency training at operational squadrons was reduced in order to ensure aircraft mission readiness.[6] Pilots took extra risks to get an ailing airplane home and airframes that would usually have been written-off were rebuilt. With French acquiescence, Israel neglected to return six Super Mystère B2s undergoing overhaul in the country. The French also sold the Israelis two superfluous Vautour IIA (one at the end of 1967 and another in August 1968), seven Super Frelons through 1969, and likely seven Alouette helicopters through 1970.

Aggravating the capabilities problem, the Fouga Magister trainers were being phased out of their secondary attack role which had proven excessively risky during the war.[7] The Americans previously agreed to some arms deliveries and was soon sending new aircraft that required absorption and training. Consequently, it was summer 1968 before the IAF felt ready to assert itself in a decisive manner.

The USA had begun selling warplanes to Israel in 1966 to balance other arm sales in the region, having already supplied Hawk SAMs. They agreed to sell A-4 Skyhawks to fill the attack role and had the appearance of a defensive system. They declined the request for F-4 Phantom IIs for dual-role heavy strike and intercept. The leading fighter-bomber of the period with tremendous capabilities, the sale would clearly have profoundly upset the military balance in the region. Later the Americans feared it would exacerbate the arms race and compel the Soviets to send even more capable offensive weapons to the Arab states.

The Americans had put a hold on all weapons-related deliveries to the region following the war. Although mostly affecting Israel, they hoped to influence others to similar restraint and contain an arms race while a peace accord was sought. Israel sent former Air Force Commander Major General Ezer Weizman, then Chief of the General Staff Division, to Washington to explain the impact of the suspension with a need to replace war losses. Israel was then expecting supply of the A-4s and UH-1 helicopters plus seeking accelerated deliveries. Given that the USSR spurned any restraint, combined with the Khartoum declaration, the embargo was lifted in late October and the requests considered.

The Israelis had been manufacturing some aircraft spares under license since the mid-1960s. These were likely those most frequently consumed and easy to manufacture. This was expanded and the defence industry took on more upgrades and remanufacturing of

The tremendous weapon load of the A-4H is illustrated by this 115 Squadron machine. Israel was not happy with the two 20mm cannon and sought to install 30mm in follow-on orders. The American warplanes also brought their multiple ejector ranks, higher electronic content, and maintenance concepts that all required adaptation by the IAF. (BIAF – Israel Aerospace Magazine)

ageing equipment. The French embargo had officially extended to spares but this was not vigorously enforced and shadow assistance helped in sustaining the equipment. The air force was also compelled to turn its attention to developing its nascent EW and SEAD capabilities to gain advantages short of introducing entirely new aircraft.

The 1966 agreement was to supply 48 new A-4Hs. These were A-4Fs with much of the 'offensive' weapons delivery capability removed including radar warning receiver (RWR) and the bombsight replaced with a more limited unit possessing a fixed gunsight. The Israelis themselves asked for the AAM capability to be removed. This left it essentially a pure attack machine and so inconsistent with IAF policy of operating multi-mission warplanes. However, it was relatively inexpensive, rugged and simple, and could carry twice the ordnance load of the Mirage at twice the endurance. The Israelis asked that a braking parachute be added as they were concerned its warplanes might have to operate from bombed runways reducing serviceable length.

From first arrival in 29 December 1967 A-4 deliveries continuing throughout 1968 to equip two squadrons. Its first strike mission was flown on 15 February. The Israelis assumed aircrew and maintainer training following return of the initial cadre from the States. With combat demands on the IAF steadily increasing, an order was placed for 52 more Hs. Deliveries began in March 1969 and ran for another year.

Concerned American willingness to sell warplanes might prove capricious, Israel worked to prolong the service of the remaining French fighter-bombers. The Super Mystères were given American and Israeli avionics and modified to take more external weapons. Their Atar engines had always suffered reliability issues with resultant crashes. Consequently, to continue operating the jets they were subjected to extensive rework fitting the Pratt & Whitney J52 turbojet from the A-4H. This increased thrust without an afterburner and so improved fuel economy while sacrificing air-to-air potency. These Sa'ar (Storm) jets were delivered at a rate of about one per month from December 1969.

The Israelis modified their squadron of Super Mystère B2s with an American engine while strengthening it to carry additional external stores. This helped sustain the valuable fighter-bomber in service despite the French embargo on military hardware. Israel devised Hebrew names for her aircraft and weapons as motivation and concealment, so the revised Super Mystère became Sa'ar. (Shlomo Aloni collection)

Beginning soon after the war the IAF began a series of upgrades to their Mirage IIICJ fleet to sustain the assets and keep them viable in a changing combat environment. Under-the-table deals with South Africa, the other famously pariah nation and Mirage operator, are reported. Changes included adding RWR, Israeli-developed weapons delivery computer, and replacing engines with the more powerful Atar 09C. The Mirages also came to carry two IR-guided (infrared) AAM routinely. This account will use the Israeli name for the Mirage, Shahak (Skyblazer), in referring to the reworked fighter. The fleet grew more diverse and seldom were two aircraft identical, complicating maintenance and operations. However, the presence of long-serving reserve cadre with deep knowledge and experience eased adverse consequences.

None of Israel's efforts at home or in America could provide interceptors the IAF urgently needed to replace Mirage losses and grow the fleet. Israel's close association with French arms industry during the 1950s and 1960s had seen her supplied with many of the most modern French armaments, often at the earliest stages of deliveries to its own forces. Israeli engineers worked shoulder-to-shoulder with their French counterparts in the development of tailor-made systems. The ultimate expression of this had Israel working with Dassault to develop a variant of the Mirage more suited to its needs.

The Mirage 5MJ used simplified avionics to include substituting a rangefinder for the large radar along with minimising the little-used night and all-weather features. The reduced volume of electronics allowed an increase in internal fuel. The wings and fuselage were 'beefed-up' for twice the external stores capacity. The increased maximum gross weight also mandated a strengthened landing gear. The jet would be easier to maintain and faster to turn between sorties. A $50 million order for 50 machines plus two dual-seat variants was placed.

The first 5MJ flew pre-war. The first production machine was completed on 12 September 1967 and initial deliveries were planned for October. The embargo nixed this. Dassault continued production in anticipation of a policy change. After reluctantly agreeing to a later delivery date the French cancelled the deal altogether following the Beirut raid. Israel maintained an indignant and vocal campaign scorning the French position and demanding delivery. They could not simply steal the jets as they did five missile boats spirited out of Cherbourg harbour on Christmas Day 1969 (see Volume 2, Chapter 4). To force the point they maintained progress payments and threatened legal action. De Gaulle was unmoved. Israel initially declined a refund but finally relented in November 1971, with the addition of an interest payment.

Israeli aviation industries proposed reverse-engineering the Mirage 5 and Atar engine for manufacture in-country as the Nesher (Eagle). This was well beyond anything these companies had undertaken. Some equipment and possibly engineering plus manufacturing support would have had to come from abroad. Still, the decision to pursue the programme was commitment to a staggering industrial and budgetary obligation for the small nation and was probably only considered because of the growing financial support from the USA and potential secret French assistance. It would still have been years before turning out aircraft. The effort was not entirely secret and stories of Israeli preparations to build a Mirage knock-off appeared in the press.

The much-vaunted Israeli foreign intelligence service appeared to provide a solution. They allegedly obtained complete manufacturing drawings and specifications for the Mirage, the powerplant, and the required machine tools. These came via a Swiss aeronautical engineer, Alfred Frauenknecht. He was an employee of Sulzer Brothers, the licensed manufacturer of the engine for the Mirage IIIS in Switzerland. One of his tasks was destruction of top-secret blueprints after their need had expired. He was induced by sympathies for the Zionist cause and $200,000 of a promised $1 million to hand over two tonnes of the documents to Israeli agents who flew the cartons to Israel. This effort was nearly complete when Frauenknecht's crime was discovered. He would be sentenced to a 4½-year prison term and the Israeli military attaché in Switzerland expelled, with others declared persona non grata.[8]

All the talk of local development and manufacturing may have been intentional misinformation. The portions of the Mirage 5MJ contract regarding engineering services, with 'parts and accessories' remained in force. These became an avenue to providing the entire aircraft in assemblies, manufactured in France by Dassault and subcontractors.[9] Significant numbers of Israeli aeronautical personnel were still working in that country during 1969 and

Although France embargoed Israel's order of 50 Mirage 5 jets, her industry assisted Israel Aircraft Industries in assembling the aircraft with jigs and assemblies built by French companies. Engines were also located and a fleet of new Mirages delivered beginning in 1971 as the Nesher. This 144 Squadron aircraft is armed with Shafrir 2 missiles and is seen at Etzion AB in Sinai with the pilot performing his walk-around inspection. (Ra'anan Weiss collection)

1970. An assembly line was set up at Israel Aircraft Industries' (IAI) Lod plant during 1969 with French-supplied tooling worth $75 million. Third parties in the transaction ensured that there was no direct French sale to Israel. The materials were flown to Israel in IAF Stratocruisers and Noratlases (often flying abroad without national markings) during low-key operations. Alternative supplies of Atars and associated spares were found offshore. France, via South Africa, is again suspected as the most likely venue.[10] A number of system changes were made from the 5MJ, although some of what has been report may be disinformation and Israeli bluster about local industrial capabilities, or unintentional confusion with later programmes.

The Israel Air Force was successful in the Six-Day War operating many dated aircraft from France. Among these was the Dassault Ouragan, first arriving in 1955. Over the following six years the battlefield would grow too lethal for the elderly warplane but it would find new use as an advanced trainer for fighter pilots streaming to the hard-pressed combat squadrons. (Ra'anan Weiss collection)

After two years of intense around-the-clock efforts the first flight of the pre-production Nesher occurred in mid-September 1969. The first production-representative machine flew on 8 January 1971. Initial deliveries to the IAF began in May of that year, operational in October though still lacking some equipment – so urgently were they needed. By late 1973 the production line had reached an output of almost three aircraft per month. The effort was so sensitive that the existence of the Nesher remained classified until 1982 and the French role decades beyond.

The Nesher was heavier on account of a 30 percent greater internal fuel volume and so considered somewhat inferior to the Mirage. The composite Mirage/Nesher squadrons, already a conglomerate of variously equipped Mirages, probably presented a challenge for their schedulers as they attempted to create flights of aircraft with compatible performance and combat systems. The first all-Nesher squadron was formed in July 1972.

Israel had persisted in efforts to obtain the F-4 Phantom, Premier Levi Eshkol making a personal appeal to the American president in early January 1968. Nearly the entire USA State and Defense Department leadership were opposed to the sale that would substantially tip the airstrike balance in Israel's favour. However, under enormous pressure from Congress and American Jewish lobbying, President Lyndon Johnson agreed in principle. He promised that the matter would be studied with a decision rendered by the end of the year. In the meantime, procurement would go ahead given long production lead-time. With Arab intransigence regarding peace negotiations, growing Soviet presence in the region with enormous arms resupply, possibly the 1968 Soviet invasion of Czechoslovakia, the French embargo, plus American election-year politics, in October the president instructed that contracts go ahead for 50 F-4Es.

Although accelerated, delivery of the Phantoms would not begin for another year. Unlike the just-under $1 million a copy Skyhawk, the Phantom ran $4.5 million – an enormous expense for the little state eased a bit with fund drives at home and abroad. This saw Jewish children, veterans, and active-duty aircrew raising money in America to buy warplanes for Israel. A large IAF cadre travelled to the States in mid-January 1969 to begin familiarisation training. The F-4 provided an order-of-magnitude increase in capabilities but demanded adoption of a new operational concept for the two-man cockpit. 'Navigators' for the back-seat weapons system officer stations were critically few for the early operational debut of the jet.[11] Pilots were cross-trained for the duty in the short-term to fill critical need.

Six pilots and four navigators returned from their USA training in July 1969, the 120 maintainers later, to form 201 Squadron by the time of initial deliveries on 5 September.[12] They also brought back knowledge of American combat tactics employed in Vietnam and how they dealt with SAMs. Aircraft arrived at a rate of four per month. The unit then had to assimilate the complex machine while training more personnel and also becoming operational – flying their first mission, a combat air patrol, on 9 October. They could not send more personnel to the USA given the demands of ongoing combat. The squadron put together a two-month course for new aircrew to include 10-day simulator sessions in Iran. However, students were being sent on combat missions before completing the training. The second squadron stood up in November. The aircraft were devoted principally to strike missions.

As the A-4 and F-4 were introduced into the force mix the Mirages and later Neshers became devoted almost exclusively to the counter-air mission from August 1968. Further efforts enhancing their air-to-ground role were shelved. Once the number of Skyhawks and Phantoms allowed, the older and less-capable French jets were operated principally in Jordan, Syria, and Lebanon in 'Tide' operations for suppression of enemy ground forces capabilities. These machines were then slowly withdrawn through 1973. All had been flown well beyond their design service lives and had grown more vulnerable over the increasingly lethal battlefields.

Although the A-4 was a fairly simple warplane it possessed more electronic systems than the IAF had previously experienced. The Phantom was another order-of-magnitude step of increasing electronic and maintenance complexity. It was one of the most sophisticated warplanes ever produced, difficult to effectively maintain and operate. Its logistical demands were prodigious. Maintenance specialists were so short for a time that American technicians had to fill in. The USA maintenance concept required some adaptation.

The new aircraft and systems brought a closer relationship between Israel and the American military and its aviation industry. At any one time there were dozens of IAF personnel in the USA training and monitoring acquisitions. The Israelis were almost fanatical about learning all they could about their weapons from the manufacturer and other operators before and after purchase, even to the point of stealing the information. They were then able to establish the true limits of performance and push the machines beyond operating manual redlines when the need arose. The information also provided data for later modifications or upgrades, often without needing to employ the expensive services of foreign manufacturers. Unlike the French, the Americans were initially more restrained in the relationship and placed conditions on sale plus use of weapons supplied, much to Israeli frustrations.

By summer 1969 the Israel Air Force was undergoing a notable transformation thanks to American patronage and nascent Israeli industrial efforts. Training requirements increased with the growing fleet and morphed with adoption of the American equipment, turbine helicopters, and 'navigators' for the F-4 back seats. Air-to-air missiles, including American models, were playing a growing role for the intercept fleet. The EW, photo-reconnaissance, and aerial refuelling (AR) fields were being addressed, sometimes as new capabilities.

With ongoing combat, Israel was seeking an unquestioned military superiority, especially in warplanes. She worked incessantly to obtain as much as she could afford and the USA would provide. In just a few years the IAF expanded 50 percent including from 250 or so combat aircraft to about 350, from nine to 14 combat squadrons, and from four to seven principal air bases. A routine of war developed by the end of 1969. Aircraft were being committed to combat so frequently that in-service rates were maintained at around 90–95 percent.[13] Missions would be sortied in the morning followed by routine squadron activities until late afternoon missions. Experience grew rapidly with increasing operations tempo.

Dealing with new and sophisticated equipment, engaging in continuous combat on three fronts, developing tactics to deal with the SAM threat, the challenge of maintain personnel quality given rapid expansion, training, and advancement, plus the slow but steady drain of experienced manpower leaving the service, made this the most turbulent period in IAF history. At any point the service was not at a tremendous numerical advantage. Yet, despite repeated protestations of being the underdog in resources and capabilities, the IAF became one of the top airpower teams in the world and certainly superior to its adversaries.

Table 11: Israeli Air Combat ORBAT, Fall 1973

Base	Unit	Aircraft	Notes
Wing 1			
Ramat David	69 Squadron	F-4E, RF-4E	operational November 1969
	109 Squadron	A-4H	operational February 1968
	110 Squadron	A-4E	to A-4s in January 1971
	117 Squadron	Shahak	upgraded Mirage IIICJs
Wing 4			
Hatzor	101 Squadron	Shahak, Nesher	Neshers from May 1971
	105 Squadron	Sa'ar	Sa'ar transition December 1969 through December 1971
	113 Squadron	Nesher	to Nesher from December 1972
	201 Squadron	F-4E	activated August 1969
Wing 8			
Tel Nof	103 Squadron	Noratlas	
	114 Squadron	Super Frelon	
	115 Squadron	A-4N	activated March 1969
	116 Squadron	A-4E, A-4H	to A-4s in January 1971
	118 Squadron	S-65	formed December 1970
	119 Squadron	F-4E, RF-4E	to F-4s in October 1970
	124 Squadron	Bell 205	to 205s beginning January 1968
Wing 10 (activated September 1972)			
Etzion	140 Squadron	A-4E	not yet operational
	144 Squadron	Nesher	operational September 1972
Base 3			
Refidim			detachments from various squadrons
Base 6			
Hatzerim	102 Squadron	A-4H	operational February 1968
	107 Squadron	F-4E	operational June 1972
	123 Squadron	Bell 205	to 205s probably October 1968
	Advanced Training Squadron	TA-4F/H/J	ancillary combat role
Base 27			
Lod	120 Squadron	C-130H, C-97, B337	C-130 added October 1971
Base 29 (operational August 1968)			
Ophir			detachments from various squadrons
Base 30			
Palmachim	200 Squadron	124I Firebee, Chukar	from August 1971

6

PENDULUM IN THE AIR

The performance of opposing air arms was notably different. Despite force composition changes, revised training, and other work undertaken by Arab defence establishments, the IDF superiority actually grew relative to its opponents. There were a variety of factors contributing to this disparity worthy of review in appreciating many of the reasons for the imbalanced combat results presented in later chapters.

Soviet arms were widely regarded as second-class compared with Western counterparts. Their exports were old models or had reduced features, referred to as 'monkey models.' The USSR scoffed at the criticisms as excuses for poor employment of the systems and lack of resolve, and there was some truth to this. Other factors were training of aircrew and boldness of airpower application by leadership.

The Egyptians, with the largest forces and national resources, and taking on the Israelis to a greater extent, adopted and adapted the aircraft as best they could. Although the Soviet machines were less complex than Western types, reliability could still be disappointing – translating to serviceability/utilisation rates. Consequently, the pace of operations demanded much support. Unable to meet the obligations represented by the many added aircraft, the UARAF began sending many outside the country for depot work, especially to East Germany and Poland. The American equipment and even the old French warplanes were generally more reliable and potent than Soviet gear.

FLIGHT TRAINING

Combat pilot training in the Arab and Israeli air forces was quite similar. After introductory lessons in light planes, primary and advanced instruction was conducted in jet trainers. Operational training was then performed using outdated combat aircraft. In the IAF this last was performed as an ancillary mission of combat units.

Egyptian expansion plans demanded growing from around 300 combat aircrew to 800 total pilots in three years to reach 1.5 per aircraft. They sought to graduate 300–400 per year. Making a pilot fully combat ready required as much as two years and a steady stream of cadets were flowing to schools that also required instructor pilots. Consequently, flight training was greatly expanded and improved.

The elderly MiG-15UTI was used extensively in training Arab pilots within air forces equipped by the Soviet Union. Once a good lead-in fighter trainer, it was becoming so dated as to leave something to be desired for those pilots transitioning to MiG-21s. The USSR long delayed providing two-seat MiG-21s. (Albert Grandolini collection)

Soviet and Indian instructors supplemented local talent – as many as 100 from the USSR and another 100 in other roles within squadrons. At least through 1970 there were four concurrent classes running, each with 60–70 students, and the curriculum was shortened from 36 to 18 months with 360–400 flight hours. The personnel demand was such that some moderately qualified individuals were taken up and a third washed out or barely qualified after training. This and the accelerated training undercut the goal of outstanding and well-trained aircrew. Just finding suitable candidates given the cultural, educational, and economic state of the country was challenging.

Training was undertaken both at home and in the USSR and included night operations. The training in Egypt was done at bases far removed from potential enemy strikes. That in the USSR including year-long courses with as many as 300 attending and three bases devoted to instruction. The Soviet syllabus and tactics were based on their modest combat experience since the Second World War. They taught rigid adherence to orders and ground controller direction – quite the opposite of the Israeli approach. It focussed on aircraft operation and little if any on manoeuvring combat and low-altitude flying. The Libyans established an Arab flight training centre to hone air-to-air and air-to-ground combat skills.

Reaching the competency and experience level of Israeli pilots would require years. Especially the Egyptians worked to improve instruction by introducing more rigorous and applicable tactical training while also flying actual combat missions. Soviet instructors sometimes accompanied UAR flights on these missions.[1] However,

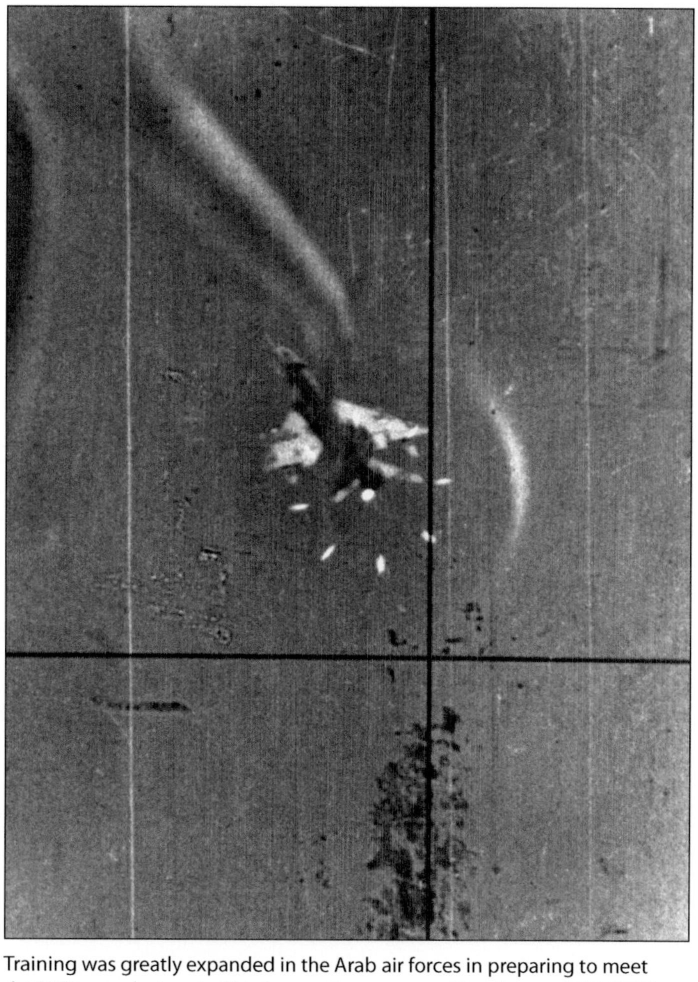

Training was greatly expanded in the Arab air forces in preparing to meet the IAF in combat again. This frame of gun camera film shows a MiG-21MF in the sights of another MiG pilot during air combat training. While these organisations worked hard, they always remained a step behind parity with the Israeli force. (David Nicolle collection)

given combat losses, experience and confidence was rebuilt only at the expense of aircrew and aircraft. With greatly increased flight hours, fatigue and errors contributed to a rise in training accidents that exceeded combat losses. The lack of two-seat MiG-21 trainers until 1968, and then slow delivery of adequate numbers, contributed to accidents as well. Losses reached such alarming levels by 1970 that the service had to back off training rigour, and flight hours decreased. The service had reached just 75 percent of its 800-pilot goal by early 1970 but counted Soviet combat pilots operating inside the country as making up the difference.

Egypt also improved realism of its combat training. Intercept scramble exercises were more numerous as were air-to-ground attack drills plus use of live munitions. She created training ranges in the western and southern deserts, and in Libya, simulating IAF airfields, HAS, AAA, Hawk sites, vehicle convoys, and more. This included firing AAM whereas the Israelis could not afford such expense.

Syrian flight training was likewise expanded with the assistance of Soviet, Pakistani, and Czech instructors, plus training in those countries. Yet, the SyAAF remained chronically short of fully qualified pilots. The Soviets found training the Syrians most challenging because of their aggressive nature and eagerness for battle despite being at an inferior state. They often lacked discipline for consistently holding to tactics. They appreciated their limitations compared with the IAF and planned only high-speed, single-pass strikes or engagements followed by rapid egress from the area. They trained little for dogfighting.

The bulk of the Jordanian pilot corps trained in Iraq and Saudi Arabia, and Pakistan lent instructors.

The growth to Israeli training eventually saw the IAF graduate more pilots in 1970 than at any time in its history and with a higher percentage of fighter pilots. Classes were increased in size and 50 additional Magister trainers acquired quietly from France and Germany. Israel considered shortening its course to hasten matriculation. They ultimately decided against this to ensure continued high quality. The number of volunteers increased given heightened standing of the air force. The candidate selection process, typically directly out of high school, and rigour of the training with an exceptionally high wash-out rate, was legendary. Their graduates normally earned wings after two years with approximately 230 flight hours, and another 40 or so before becoming qualified squadron aircrew. Another change was to send only experienced pilots back as instructors rather than junior personnel just completing operational flight training.

During these years the young pilots matured quickly given the high operations pace with opportunity for combat experience. All were logging more flight time annually than pre-war with at least the Israeli and Egyptian fighter pilots flying comparable hours during the period.[2] For the Israelis, accidents in all manner of training summed to an average of more than 10 airplanes destroyed per year, owing partially to undisciplined flying.[3] Given the difficulty in acquiring replacement aircraft, this should have been confronted with greater vigour than evident.

INTERCEPTORS

The principal Arab interceptor, the MiG-21, had initially been designed to attack bombers at high altitude with AAM and so was a compromise solution. The MiG-21F-13s from the war had a 30mm cannon but with just 30 rounds expended within two seconds at a rate less than the Mirage with its two cannon. It carried two AAM plus a belly tank while the Mirage could accommodate up to three tanks along with a pair of AAM. Endurance was comparatively short, and the tank greatly undermined performance and manoeuvrability. The cockpit was cramped with poor vision to the rear. Handling deteriorated above 500 knots. The new jets were MiG-21PFS and MiG-21FLs that lacked guns, possessed rudimentary navigation systems, were heavier, had high fuel consumption and low acceleration at low altitude, and could carry only minimal external stores. Most combat missions ended at a critical fuel state with many pilots diverting, landing on fumes, and a few having to abandon their jet. Egyptian workshops developed a higher capacity drop tank after the Soviets proved uncooperative. They also adapted some FL and PF jets to take an Indian 23mm gun pod. The USSR began delivering the MiG-21PFM variant in early 1969 that added back a cannon, possessed better radar and gunsight, and featured RWR. The MF model had a 23mm cannon with a good load of shells, could carry three external tanks, and had four hardpoints for R-3S AAM. However, the radar was of such poor performance and high failure rates that the pilots still had to rely upon GCI. Fortunately, the jet could also receive uplinked GCI data for non-voice intercept vectors. The MiG had vulnerabilities that caused it to 'flame' and explode with a few cannon shell hits.

The Israelis relied on the Fouga Magister for training up to and including advanced instruction, leaving lead-in to operational units employing, initially, single-seat Ouragans and later two-seat Skyhawks. While the instructors could imagine a better scheme, it was producing fine pilots and finances did not allow for alternative equipment. (Author's collection)

Israel's French-built Mirage IIICJ fighters remained their principal interceptor, jettisoning the air-to-ground mission, and enjoyed great success against the Soviet-built MiG-21. The high level of IAF pilot experience as well as superior technology played a large role in this achievement. The Israelis proudly displayed the kills achieved by the aircraft on the port side of the nose, getting quite cluttered on some of the machines. (Albert Grandolini collection)

The Mirage manoeuvred about as well as the MiG-21 but enjoyed greater endurance and acceleration. Its radar was poor and unreliable, replaced with ballast in many of the jets while some were retained for night engagements. Intercepts relied principally upon GCI vectoring. At high g's the gyro for the gunsight could malfunction and cause the reticle to sink out of sight. When this happened it became almost pure chance to score a cannon hit. The aircraft was a fine performer and with the 30mm cannon each possessing 125 rounds (seven-seconds firing).

By summer 1970 the F-4s had reached numbers where they began appearing in air-to-air engagements. It had superior speed and good manoeuvrability, the latter enhanced with wing slats in later deliveries. Turn performance was comparable though it bled energy fast and was not as nimble as the interceptors. The 20mm Gatling gun gave high rate of fire and 630 rounds for six-seconds of firing. The Phantom carried up to four each infrared- and radar-guided AAM.[4] Persistence was superior with greater fuel capacity despite the two engines that also improved survivability. The crew of two reduced workload and added a pair of eyes for tracking adversaries along with the effective radar. The black exhaust smoke aided enemy locating the fighter.

The MiG-21 could out-run the Mirage but not a Phantom. The IAF practiced a 'let-him-pass' manoeuvre in which the pilot abruptly slowed the jet with throttle and speedbrakes such that the enemy overshot and the Israeli could readily get on his tail. The Arabs developed a similar manoeuvre in which they abruptly pitched up to get the MiG-21 to near-zero airspeed such that the adversary overshot during which the MiG pitched down to a superior firing position.

Israel developed and manufactured the infrared-guided Shafrir and these were employed during the war, though with disappointing results.[5] The 45kg (99lb) missile had a range of 2km (1.2mi) and its electronics were such that it could only be fired within an off-boresight angle of 30 degrees and with the target not manoeuvring beyond 2g. The 2.0kg (4.4lb) warhead was woefully small. The missile went on to score just two kills. The IAF also adopted R-3Ss and launchers found in captured stocks at Bif Gifgafa but never scored with them either (though they did damage a few aircraft). Israeli pilots considered the Shafrir and R-3S to be of such low effectiveness that some fired these outside engagement envelopes simply to 'clean-up' the jet before closing to gunfire range.

The improved Shafrir 2 began supplanting the original (carried into 1970) in July 1969 with 12kg (27lb) warhead, 2.5km (1.6mi) range, and off-boresight raised to 45 degrees against a target manoeuvring up to 5g. It was immediately successful. However, the warhead had a delayed-fuse detonator optimised for MiG-21 engagement and so tended to explode too far aft of the hotter-burning engine of the Su-7 until corrected. The Shafrirs were also integrated onto the Sa'ars and reconnaissance Vautours for a defensive capability such that fighter escort would not be essential.

The USA permitted Israel to buy the essentially equivalent but more mature AIM-9B missile in 1968. The first AIM-9B kills were scored by Mirages in early 1969. The AIM-9D apparently came with the F-4Es, E and H models likely delivered in early 1970. This AAM was integrated into the Mirage in mid-July 1970 at the instigation of a squadron commander.[6] Bought initially to ensure sufficient AAM rounds given slow Shafrir delivery rate, the Sidewinder was

Syrian fighter pilot Mohammad Mansour developed what was called the zero-airspeed manoeuvre, in later decades the cobra manoeuvre. As illustrated here it involves an abrupt pitched up to rapidly bleed speed then pitch back down. Like the Israeli 'let-him-pass' manoeuvre this could cause an adversary closing from the rear to overshoot and then find his intended victim on his tail. (Diagram by Tom Cooper)

The Israeli-developed Shafrir IR-guided AAM had done poorly in its initial incarnation. The Shafrir 2, shown under the wing of a Mirage, was essentially equivalent to an upgraded American AIM-9B and reasonably reliable. It scored respectably during the War of Attrition. (Ra'anan Weiss collection)

more reliable and effective. Later models offered progressively better manoeuvrability and off-boresight engagement plus superior seekerhead, greatly out-performing the AAM available to the Arab forces. Still, the missiles were in short supply and the Mirages occasionally flew with just one round. The IAF achieved 21 percent hit rate overall with IR-guided AAM.[7] The Phantom's proven radar and AIM-7 Sparrow missile system gave a beyond-visual-range and all-weather air-to-air dimension. However, the AIM-7Es arriving with the F-4Es were then of low effectiveness.

The AAM supplied by the USSR was the K-13A or R-3S (NATO AA-2A 'Atoll', a reverse-engineered AIM-9B). It was uninspiring, suffering low reliability and effectiveness. It could not be fired at more than 2.5g or against targets manoeuvring at more than 3g. The infrared source discrimination by the warhead was poor, easily confused by environmental sources. Failure rate was high and hit ratio likely less than 10 percent.[8]

Kill rates for the latest AAM employed by the IAF were approximately 60 percent and the fighter pilots were gaining confidence in the capability. As air battles grew larger, AAM offered the opportunity for kills at longer range and without the time-consuming closing to gun range during which an adversary could also close. The IAF adapted and by the end of the War of Attrition more kills were being scored with missiles than guns. Arab fighter pilots were trained to employ AAM in set-piece engagements unsuited for the theatre. The UARAF fired many missiles and shells at IAF aircraft that failed to bring down the target, and then had to hastily extricate from the fight. The Israelis could usually dictate favourable terms for an engagement.

Training and disciplined adherence to tactics played a role. The Egyptians were more rigid in this, especially in flight-pairs remaining together. The Syrians were 'cowboys' and flew almost recklessly from the Soviet perspective. Both could be disadvantages in certain circumstances. The Israelis often broke formation and fought one-on-one. While this occasionally led to unfavourable outcomes, especially when the adversary had more airplanes in the fight as became more common by 1970, they assessed that the fluid application of tactics meeting unique circumstances remained the best approach. The pair might separate but remain coordinated and there were seldom the resources for larger formations. They judged the Egyptian adherence to pairs

Israeli ground personnel service the AIM-9D and AIM-7E AAM beneath an IAF F-4E. The AIM-9D was the standout best IR-guided missile in the theatre and its arrival with the Phantoms was a significant boon. The AIM-7E was welcomed with its radar-guided, beyond-visual-range capability but engagement was more complicated and success rate much lower. (Ra'anan Weiss collection)

The Soviet R-3S was a copy of the AIM-9B but performed poorly by comparison given less reliable electronics. Improved models were slow coming to Arab combatants and so they were significantly disadvantaged in air-to-air combat. (Tom Cooper and Amr Safadi collections)

as simplifying the attackers' task in that they essentially fought one jet at a time.

Under the circumstances presented in preceding paragraphs it is reasonable to expect the IAF enjoying a greatly disproportionate air-to-air exchange ratio. Witness the same with UN and North Korean jet combat, Germany versus the USSR in the early years of their Second World War combat, and USA versus Japanese aircraft in the later stages of that conflict. Believing Israeli success was principally due to a Mirage squadron manned by only the best IAF pilots (a false conclusion), some UARAF officers proposed doing the same. Such a unit had a better chance to shift the equation and increase enemy losses. The proposal was repeatedly rejected.

Some in the Arab air forces, and later Soviets, believed the key to the IAF's success lay not in training and experience but in the machine, especially the Mirage, or by mercenary pilots and technicians from Western countries, potentially with Vietnam experience. Several attempts to buy Mirages were undertaken, but these deals always fell through. The USSR, either for their own intelligence collection or to convince the Arabs that it was not a 'fantastical creature', sought in summer 1969 to bribe a Lebanese pilot to fly one of his country's Mirages to Baku, Azerbaijan. This was reported and the two diplomats, one wounded during the confrontation with police, were expelled. The Libyans, greatly expanding its forces after a 1969 coup, bought Mirage 5s that were clearly meant to support any Egyptian effort against the Israelis as they were excess to Libyan defence needs.[9] Pilots from many Arab states travelled to Libya to participate in dissimilar air combat manoeuvre training against the Mirages to learn the best means of engaging the jet. France also provided Mirage III conversion training to Egyptian pilots carrying Libyan passports.

FIGHTER-BOMBERS

The USSR fighter-bombers provided to the Arabs were inferior to the Western airframes operated by the Israelis in many vital respects. These had generally been developed originally to counter American nuclear-armed bombers and were not ideally suited to tactical combat. Range, payload, and speed were deficient, and weapon delivery accuracy comparatively poor given lagging electronic capabilities. The navigation systems were rudimentary. These factors attributed somewhat to the disparity in scope of combat missions flown and combat success. By 1973 the Egyptians counted IAF daily ordnance delivery capacity at 3.3-times that

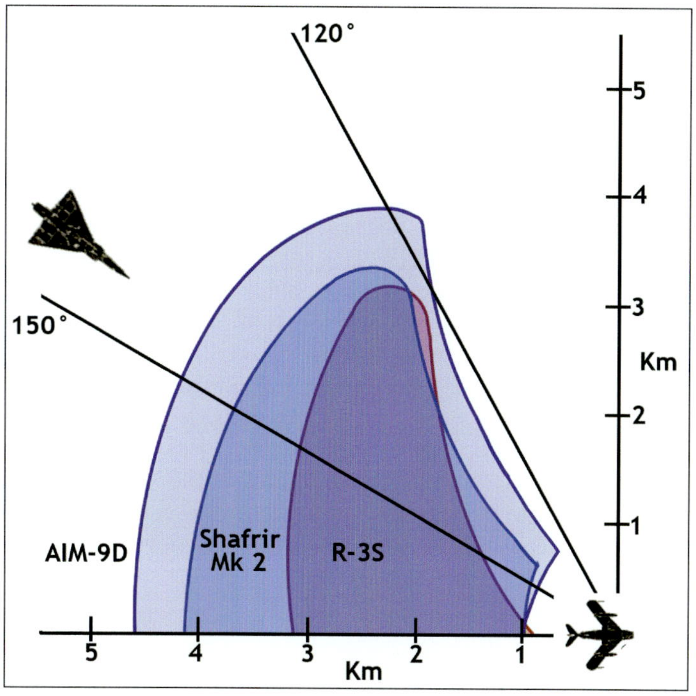

This diagram illustrates the significant engagement envelope advantages of the Israeli Shafrir 2 (AIM-9B similar) and American AIM-9D Sidewinder over the Soviet R-3S Vympel air-to-air missile. The Soviet missile appears comparable but reliability and seekerhead performance were so poor that it seldom met this envelope or struck the target. Additionally, Western AAM could be launched from an aircraft or against targets manoeuvring at higher normal load factors (g). (Diagram by Tom Cooper)

The success of Israeli pilots flying Mirage IIICJ fighters, evidently a far superior jet to the Soviet machines in Arab inventories, brought forth great desire among the Arab air forces to examine the Dassault product if not adopt the aircraft themselves. Arab pilots were permitted to perform familiarisation training on the jet in France while Soviet agents tried to bribe a Lebanese pilot to defect with one of his country's Mirage IIIEL examples (shown). The plot was foiled in summer 1969. (Albert Grandolini collection)

of the combined frontline Arab states (760 tonnes in the best of circumstances).[10]

The elderly MiG-17F had only agility and a periscope to protect it in air-to-air combat, though its 37mm and twin 23mm cannon could be deadly if brought to bear on an opponent. In its principal air-to-ground role it would commonly carry a pair of 100kg (220lb) bombs and eight 80mm rockets plus two external tanks. The Su-7BMK possessed good speed and acceleration but relatively poor climb rate. Manoeuvrability at high speed was discouraging. The two 30mm cannon lent a powerful punch. Depending on range sought, payload could be four 500kg (1,100lb) or six 250kg (550lb) bombs, or a variety of rocket pods.

Squadrons in the Nile Delta could hope only to attack targets in the far west of Sinai and with a meagre bomb load delivered with medium accuracy. After a low-altitude ingress to a target area if the pilot did not locate the objective on pop-up the mission was abandoned and the flight returned immediately. Only approximately nine minutes over Sinai was allowed owing to minimal fuel reserves and IAF interceptor reaction time. Stores were found wanting in terms of reliability and high drag. The Soviets delivered only enough bombs and rockets to support a few days of fighting. They refused to supply parachute-retarded and napalm bombs. Egypt worked to adopt a variety of other weapons, some of their own manufacture, to the aircraft. They added more hardpoints to the Su-7BMK and Egyptian external tanks helped with range/endurance. However, the other detractors meant that these were minor enhancements.

The Il-28 bomber was so dated and vulnerable that any attempt to use it in attacking Israeli targets was tantamount to suicide. The machines were, at best, trainers and employed in sea patrol. The newer Tu-16 held more advantages but their chances of penetrating the Israeli interceptor screen to reach meaningful targets was minimal. They initially lacked standoff weapons.

By contrast, Israeli strike jets flew from bases in central Israel with more bombs delivered with greater accuracy. The aging French aircraft were modest attackers but still superior to Soviet equipment. The introduction of the A-4 and then F-4 tipped this balance further.

The A-4 carried up to three external tanks, though possessing good range regardless. Weapons load was up to 3,700kg (8,200lb) with a wide variety of stores and acceptable delivery accuracy as the A-4Hs were initially delivered (improved later). The Israelis were working to replace the twin 20mm cannon with 30mm. The jet possessed remarkable manoeuvrability to evade intercept. It was relatively easy to fly and maintain. The F-4E's typical combat range was 1,290km (800mi) with up to three external tanks. The radar supported effective all-weather navigation. The 7,258kg (16,000lb) weapons load and delivery accuracy was unmatched. Israel also adopted American bombs, slowly displacing the locally produced weapons, and on USA multiple ejector racks. 'Snakeye' high-drag bombs were supplied but Israel initially had to manufacture its own napalm and cluster bombs. Rockets continued to be used by French jets and Skyhawks.

By October 1973 the IAF had progressively increased its weapons payload capacity some four-fold compared with May 1967 – from 570 tonnes per day to 2,000. Lethality against ground targets increased 12.5 times due largely to navigation and attack electronic systems that increased bombing accuracy by a factor of 3.5 over earlier generation systems.[11]

With the new nav/attack systems in the American jets came new tactics. Bomb-toss delivery supplemented the familiar level or dive-bombing methods. Skyhawks became known for the 'Indian circle' attack pattern with a pair of jets circling the target and alternately diving in to attack. One aircraft was always opposite the attacker looking for threats. In attacking SAMs, many tactics were tried by the Phantoms until settling on an extremely low-level ingress followed by a pop-up scissors to dive onto the battery in a funnel zone above in which the missiles could not engage. Destroying the radar and guidance control trailers was primary, rendering the missiles useless. Bombing even an empty site made it unusable in housing a battery. For Arab attackers meeting Hawk batteries the principal tactic was ingress and egress from the target area at exceptionally low altitude – although this was where the performance and flying qualities of their combat aircraft were deficient.

ELECTRONIC WARFARE

Arab forces had little if any experience with EW before the war and were slow correcting the deficit. The Soviets initially provided little if any such gear mounted on the aircraft and so the Egyptians and Syrians fought without alerting and self-protection systems. Even the basic ground-based barrage jammers of enemy communications and radar were minimal and played little role. Under Riadh the army and ADC began to address all aspects of EW, especially communications, with a committee under the President's Scientific Advisor, Professor Salah Hidayat, beginning work on 24 June 1967 and continuing until an Electronic War Administration was created in 1970.[12] Countermeasures against the Hawk SAM and radar-directed AAA was almost non-existent or little employed. The Egyptian counted as war assets the Soviet-operated EW aircraft in the country, principally supporting USSR Mediterranean operations. The Egyptians may have considered seeking Western equipment to meet urgent needs.[13] Only in April 1970 did the USSR send to Egypt for field tests the experimental Smalta, heliborne system to jam Hawk guidance, and truck-based Takan for jamming aircraft radar.[14] The Soviets held these close to the chest. If it was at risk of falling into Israeli hands the equipment was to be blown-up. They also deployed ground-based electronic counter-countermeasures (ECCM) against Israeli jammers employed during SAM attacks. Egypt set up its first EW department in August 1970 and began building capability.[15]

Israeli EW capabilities were initially modest but meaningful given Arab vulnerabilities. They used barrage jammers to confound enemy voice communications and radar, some of these integrated into attack jets. Before the war they had acquired a French Thompson-CSF 'Alligator' stand-off noise jammer in aircraft pods. Dubbed Yabelet (Wart), these required an on-board operator and so were integrated onto the two-seat Vautour IINs. It was intended to defeat Soviet SAMs and surveillance radar but the effectiveness against the S-75 is difficult to assess from available literature. For lower-speed and standoff scenarios, palletised systems may also have been carried by transports to include ELINT (frequencies identification and emitter geo-location). Transports were also equipped to dump chaff. Other jamming and electronic emission collection/analysis assets were ground-based. Mobile EW stations were also developed, presumably positioned near the front ahead of a SEAD raid.

With the monumental growth in extent and complexity of air defences, Israeli EW expanded to match. ELINT reconnaissance became increasingly important as bombing raids demanded data on enemy radar and missile guidance transmissions for suitable jamming, and to plot safe routes through the defences. To contribute in this increasingly complex and dangerous environment various EW systems were apparently added to most of the Vautours owing to their excess internal volume plus power and cooling capacity for the 'black boxes.' These were effective, the Egyptians complaining to the Soviets about the vulnerability if their radar net to the jamming. Yabelet continued to evolve to include capabilities against the advanced S-75 and S-125 SAMs. Another podded system called Grapevine followed to meet evolving opposition systems. After retirement of the Vautours in 1972, or before, Skyhawks reportedly carried the pods.

Since the fronts were comparatively narrow, jamming of tracking radar could be narrowly focussed to support SEAD strikes. Placing such systems aboard assault helicopters and C-47s was one such

Right: This Yabelet (Wart) jammer pod was photographed in a museum display beside the Vautour bomber that initially employed it. Two of these systems were carried at a time, with perhaps as few as four ever acquired. The electronics, generator airscrew, and cooling apertures are fitted into a 1,300-litre external tank. The innards were a French Thompson-CSF 'Alligator' jammer. (Author)

Below: The Vautour IIN was favoured for carrying the Yabelet jamming pods given its two seats, the rear crewman operating the gear. The ageing Vautour retained value throughout the conflict but losses, both combat and mishaps, gradually wore away the small fleet with no potential for replacement. This 110 Squadron aircraft carries kill markings on the tail for aircraft destroyed on the ground during the recent war. (BIAF – Israel Aerospace Magazine)

solution as they could fly low and slow for extended periods. The Katef (Shoulder) system was developed with emitters in a bank that fit into the troop doors of these aircraft.[16]

The USA provided intelligence on the S-75 and also electronic countermeasures (ECM) equipment to outfit some of the fighters. The earliest delivery of ECM for this purpose may have been in early January 1970, possibly preceding commencement of deep strikes in Egypt (see Volume 2, Chapter 4).[17] During the intense SEAD operations in summer 1970 the Americans provided ECM pods for the Phantoms that had been developed for Vietnam combat. The F-4Es were equipped with RWR that could likely be adjusted to warn of the various emissions from the changing air defence systems. The EW modifications for perhaps two Stratofreighters probably included ECM to jam enemy systems in support of fighter-bomber strikes, 'snooping' to determine the nature and location of enemy emitters, and communications-intercepts (communications intelligence, COMINT), augmenting capabilities from other aircraft such as Dakotas. SIGINT came via a C-97 from the United States Air Force (USAF) in 1969 or 1970.

Following the ceasefire on the canal, efforts to find a solution to the enemy defences received considerable attention. Work continued to refine Katef and transport-based systems to extend their capabilities. An airborne EW organisation, Unit 555, was formed for such missions. Where these home-grown capabilities did not keep pace with threats, the IAF purchased additional EW pods from the Americans for the F-4Es, or at least those the USA would release and Israel could afford. Possibly not the latest and best systems, they were important additions that expanded EW expertise. Flare and chaff dispensers also began to be adopted, paced by funding.

PHOTO-RECONNAISSANCE

Egyptian PR was marginal to rudimentary as dictated by fleet aircraft and camera equipment (or no camera at all). The first dedicated PR squadron was created in October 1967. Several MiG-21s and Su-7s were given internal cameras, or cameras installed in modified external tanks that became operational in 1968. The USSR eventually delivered several examples of the MiG-21RF, a PR-variant. Capabilities continued to lag those of Israel with respect to airspeed, range, imaging aspect, and photo quality. This situation and the modest capabilities of other intelligence gathering means meant that targeting data for national decision-making, gunners, and strike squadrons left much to be desired. Syrian capabilities were nil.

Arab PR capabilities were minimal to none for many years owing principally to Soviet failure to provide the resources. Frustrated by this, Egypt moved on its own and modified the MiG-21's 490-litre centreline external tank to take a camera. Here two employees of Helwan Aircraft Factory perform such an installation. (Tom Cooper collection)

Israeli fast photo-reconnaissance had always been vital supporting penetration of enemy airspace and intelligence collection. They possessed two Mirage IIICJ(R)s with special camera noses. Of diminishing value were the two remaining Vautour IIBRs. One on such a mission was downed by AAA on 1 December 1967 demonstrating the growing vulnerability. As the Arab air defences

An Israeli Stratofreighter given EW modifications was KC-97F 38 'Megiddo' (51-0378) which began serving in 1968. The multiple added antennae and fairings attest to the role, all subject to revision. The large aircraft, though aged and cantankerous, had the volume and electrical system capacity to support the mission. (BIAF – Israel Aerospace Magazine)

became more proficient, fighter sorties in one area would distract defences while the recce jet quickly executed its pass. By June 1970 the threat was so grave that only inferior oblique photographs of the SAM array across the canal was possible. This was provided by the same fast jets as well as transports with oblique photography capabilities flying along the borders. The photo-Mirage team then adopted partial-pressure suits permitting flight above 18,300m (60,000ft), beyond the reach of S-75s. Jamming of the SAMs were conducted concurrently.

When the Israelis were finally permitted to purchase the Phantom they lost no time in ordering six photo-reconnaissance examples. The RF-4Es began arriving in 1971 and, unlike the standard recce models, these were equipped to fire AIM-9s. Their radar and photo-flash flare cartridge dispensing systems bolstered night reconnaissance. These powerful jets carried a far more extensive and sophisticated suite of cameras than the Mirages. The USAF helped the Israelis set up a photo processing centre.[18]

The earliest missions for the RF-4s were to monitor disposition of Egypt and Syria's air defences arrayed along the fronts. These defences became so lethal by summer 1970 as to make recce penetrations extremely hazardous. Flights were conducted at 600 knots and at such a low altitude that the major hazards were birds and fishing boat masts. It is believed Israel ceased PR flights across the Suez missile batteries that summer, and across the Purple Line on the Golan Heights in summer 1972. However, missions to image other areas of those countries were undertaken by skirting the SAM 'belts.' The Egyptians (plus Soviets) and Syrians became increasingly more aggressive challenging these sorties – escorted partially or fully along their route – until each mission risked a major air battle. Consequently, oblique photography was reemphasised with two Stratofreighters modified to carry exceptionally large cameras. One of these, borrowed from the Americans, was a giant one-of-a-kind unit of extraordinary capability and requiring a major modification for installation. It served for about three years in the early 1970s before the camera was returned.

The Israelis had been for many years interested in the American's Long Range Oblique Photography camera with rotating prism assembly for photography out either side of the jet. This remarkable but exceptionally large and heavy unit could resolve a 25 centimetre (10 inch) object at 37km (23mi). After much delay the USA finally sold Israel the enormous G-139 pod containing a 680kg (1,500lb) unit. Acquired in October 1971, the Israelis carried the pod on the centreline of RF-4s and on two specially modified F-4Es.

The USA also lent Israel what was subsequently advertised as the world's largest camera, to be employed for oblique photography out of a Stratofreighter. The 2,950kg (6,500lb), 240inch focal length unit with 18x36inch negative could purportedly resolve a golf ball from 13,700m (45,000ft) altitude. Shown in a museum display, this 'W33' monster had previously been carried by an American RB-36 and a C-97. Inserting it into one of the IAF's KC-97s required a major modification performed at the General Dynamics plant in Fort Worth, Texas. (Author)

After much effort Israel was able to convince the USA to sell a podded version of their remarkable Long Range Oblique Photography camera as the unique G-139. Shown beneath its carrier aircraft, an F-4E, the massive size of the 1,810kg (4,000lb) store with marginal ground clearance is evident. It significantly degraded the performance of the Phantom. (Author)

Like the Mirages forced to exceptionally high altitude by the SAMs, the Phantoms RF-4Es also had to operate up to 22,250m (73,000ft), requiring the aircrew to also wear partial-pressure suits. The encumbered navigator is seen boarding aircraft 199 of 119 Squadron with much assistance. (Ofer Zidon collection)

ASSAULT HELICOPTERS AND SPECIAL OPERATORS

Arab assault helicopter forces were significantly improved with addition of Mi-8s that bolstered commando insertions and extractions. It took time to assimilate the aircraft and train with them. This heavy-lift machine with drop-down loading ramp was respected for its internal capacity, but performance in the region's climate left something to be desired. The range versus payload equation usually meant a reduced commando team during operations into Sinai. Neither Arab nor Israeli aviators had night-vision goggles and so relied upon moonlight for ground reference, limiting the number of nights available for operations.

Israel enjoyed more capable helicopters. The Sikorsky S-58s and H-34s were the principal assault rotorcraft. These piston-powered machines were comparatively limited and struggled in the hot climate. The turboshaft-powered Super Frelons were showing the potential of the new generation that Israel was eager to take advantage of. These heavy lift machines had proven their value in the war, supporting fast-moving advances, and were invaluable in the continuing conflict with extensive specops. Parts were acquired from the French for a time longer before Israel sought sources wherever they could be found.

The US Army had made significant strides in establishing turbine helicopter warfare doctrine during the Southeast Asia conflict and had developed some outstanding machines. Both were shared with the IDF. For the medium transport 'choppers' the very successful UH-1 'Huey' was ordered. With sliding doors on both sides of the cabin these could be loaded much more easily and troops could dismount more quickly. The turbine engine offered improved performance with greater interior and sling load capacity. Speed, manoeuvrability, and the landing skids were all superior to the Sikorsky.

The USA permitted supply of a commercial model, the Bell 205, although this was essentially a UH-1D. Israel's first examples were supplied via Italy with 22 new Agusta-Bell 205s delivered starting in December 1967. Jordan complained about the sale and America accused Italy of proceeding without approval. Twenty-nine Bell 205As (UH-1Ds and UH-1Hs) were then acquired directly from the States. Military equipment was installed by Israel with rescue winches, flare and smoke grenade tubes, and door guns with the Belgian 7.62mm FN MAG. The 205s displaced the S-58s in spring 1968 as the principal helicopter.

Acquiring additional such resources became a priority especially in supporting growing sayerot specops teams with their high operations tempo. With the new American willingness to supply Israel, the Sikorsky CH-53 Sea Stallion became the choice. This upped capacity to 55 troops or 1.5 tonnes internally, loaded across the rear ramp, and large loads transported via sling. Range, capacity, and speed were superior to the Mi-8. They were also fitted with armour, external fuel tanks, and rescue winch. Seventeen were

During this period, as the USA supplied military aircraft to Israel, some were sold as supposed commercial products – though this fooled no one. Among these was the Agusta-Bell 206A JetRanger supplied from Italy but with certain American approval. The aircraft were easily militarised and were placed into service with the air force as liaison and scout helicopters. (BIAF – Israel Aerospace Magazine)

supplied as commercial S-65C-3s virtually identical to the CH-53D. This procurement was also greatly debated in the USA government before go-ahead, with the State Department opposed but President Johnson approving.

The first of the heavy choppers arrived in October 1969 on-board C-5A airlifters. As with most new weapons obtained by the IDF, training and other preparations had preceded arrival of hardware, and the helicopters were almost immediately in operational status.

As Israel moved to American equipment, with each new type possessing a different internal capacity, repeated and frustrating shifts in the size of squads to be carried were necessary. However, the machines' greater performance offered new potential that was soon being exploited. For example, 250kg (550lb) and 500kg (1,100lb) 'sprinkler bomb' explosive devices and mines had been devised for delivery by the helos, carried as sling loads and their carrying cables activating the delayed-action fuses as the helicopters pulled away.

AIRDROP

Airdrop was rare in the region, apart from paratrooper support all possessed, with Israel the clear leader. It relied upon the transport fleet of Noratlases, ageing Stratocruisers and, from October 1971, two of the far more capable C-130Hs. The new airlifter also supported off-field assault landings. Apart from parachute-recovered airdrop the IAF was also becoming adept at low altitude parachute extraction system delivery of vehicles and guns.

AERIAL REFUELLING

Only Israel was able to introduce in-flight refuelling during the period. American fighter-bombers came equipped for aerial refuelling, although Israel had no immediate means of employing the capability. The value lay in extending mission range and endurance to get the most from limited resources. A complication was that Skyhawks were equipped for probe-and-drogue AR while the Phantoms had a receptacle for boom refuelling.

America was at first loath to provide tankers or even the equipment to create a tanker. Yet, early in A-4 deliveries they permitted sale of D-704 centreline buddy-refuelling hose reel pods. The initial Skyhawk cadre were trained in the States to AR and they returned to train others. The maiden AR contact by an A-4 in Israel occurred on 6 June 1968. Although a marginal capability, these pods were put to immediate use enhancing combat missions.

One of Israel's KC-97s was modified by IAI to mount a D-704 under each wing. The modification required wing strengthening, fuel system alteration, and system control wiring, illustrating the growing capabilities of Israeli aerospace industries. The first AR from the KC-97 was in June 1968. The fact that this is the same month as the first Skyhawk-to-Skyhawk buddy-refuelling, and the KC-97 modification was many months long, suggests that the pods were delivered earlier than the airplanes. It again bespeaks quiet American assistance helping Israel achieve its AR aspirations with a tanker available soon after the Skyhawks became operational.

Aircrew began qualification training for AR, both buddy and tanker. The capabilities were operational in early 1970 but not

Left: Israel's squadron of Noratlas transports supported both paratrooper and cargo airdrop. The latter, demonstrated here and a capability little addressed by the Arab forces. The Nords were invaluable in moving freight and personnel to Sinai destinations. Their continued trips to France to collect equipment and spares was done in a low-key fashion. (IAF)

Below: One of the IAF's two C-130Hs, acquired in late 1971, is seen during a demonstration of airland operations offloading a paratroop assault team. The Hercules, with its turboprop engines and high reliability, was vital in modernising the transport fleet. However, the chronically cash-strapped Zahal were buying the airplanes at a very slow rate. (Author's collection)

Left: Israel's new warplanes from the USA came with aerial refuelling capabilities that initially could not be used. The exception were the A-4s that were supplied with a number of 'buddy' refuelling pods (here an A-4E refuels a TA-4J) and the initial cadre of pilots trained for AR in the United States. The capability was employed operationally but evidently rarely. (Ra'anan Weiss collection)

Below: Instead of employing a valuable fighter-bomber as a tanker, and with its modest 'give away' fuel quantity, Israel developed a tanker with two of the Skyhawk's AR pods installed under the wings of this KC-97G to produce an experimental tanker – here refuelling a pair of 115 Squadron A-4Hs. The tanker was flying from 1968 until destroyed in a ground accident in 1970. (Ofer Zidon collection)

routinely employed. During some operations, A-4s were dedicated to AR patrols with the buddy pods if needed. Unfortunately, the tanker was lost in a ground mishap during November 1970. Two additional 97s were modified for the role in 1971 to 1972 with pods from the United Kingdom company Flight Refuelling. The IAF also began developing a probe AR capability for the F-4 in 1970 as a locally designed modification. This was slowly added to aircraft from 1971. They acquired probes for the S-65s but, except for some trials with a Noratlas, had no compatible tanker.

GROUND-BASED AIR DEFENCES

Defences against air attack included SAMs and AAA (some radar-directed) and other antiaircraft guns. Guns had been the greatest bane of aircraft engaged in ground attack during the war whereas missiles played little role. Systems reliant upon signals from separate radar and control elements were largely hardwire-based and the cables were subject to cutting by enemy action.

One serious Arab deficiency was little use of Identification Friend-or-Foe (IFF). While the transponders were usually installed, it was either not trusted or not routinely operated. Friendly fire incidents resulted. Airspace control and coordination clearly demanded improvement. Egypt had to rely on spotters and landline communications to help separate enemy from friendly aircraft and give early warning of low-flying aircraft. After the 17 June 1969 Israeli sonic boom over Cairo (see Volume 2, Chapter 2), spotters were increased to a double ring around the city and equipped with radios. Israel did the same in reporting low-flying aircraft over the front undetectable by radar but had a superior radar network in the area and dependable IFF.

Antiaircraft guns and artillery were deployed in the hundreds with approximately half radar-directed. Arab forces employed a variety with among some of the more common systems including the single-barrel 57mm AAA firing at 105–120 rounds per minute (rpm) and twin 23mm. The tracked ZSU-23-4 Shilka, dating from

Small and simple weapons could be quite effective against low-flying airplanes and helicopters. The Oerlikon 20mm cannon was used in many applications including this simple single-weapon mount for ground operation. A Lebanese gunner helps defend an airfield where a Mirage becomes airborne. (Albert Grandolini ocllection)

1965, carried four 23mm guns in the turret of an armoured vehicle. Gun-laying was either optical or via the on-board radar. Targets could be detected at 20km (12mi) and effective range was 3km (1.9mi). It was especially effective at low altitude with a dense concentration of fire up to 3,400–4,000rpm.

Jordan relied on towed quad-mount 12.7mm guns and the tracked M-42 vehicles with twin 40mm cannon. Their gunners seemed to enjoy greater success than Egyptians in bringing down Israeli jets. Jordan adopted 14 fire units of manually guided British Tigercat short-range SAMs in 1969 that they soon found unsatisfactory.

With greater integration of early warning and air defence in Israel it became advisable in 1969 to move the Air Defence Forces under the IAF and this was completed in 1970. Initially with some 53 AAA batteries, these were heavily reliant on reservists. Some 60–80 percent of the systems were visually directed, the exceptions being radar-directed 40mm units. With the borders 'hot' since the war and the static army positions in Sinai subject to quick air attack by the UARAF, there was need for lighter and mobile anti-aircraft defences. In 1969 IAI developed a dual 20mm cannon installation of the American M-55 quad .50-cal anti-aircraft gun system from the Second World War. Hundreds of these TCM-20s were manufactured from 1970 as either towed or vehicle-mounted systems, the latter on M-3 halftracks plus captured BTR-152 and Al-Walid vehicles. Each gun had a 60-round magazine and the system fired at 1,200-1,400rpm. By October 1973 the IAF possessed perhaps 100 AAA batteries, 20 percent radar-directed.

The 57mm S-60 anti-aircraft gun was among the most common in the Arab arsenals. Supplied in the hundreds by the Soviet Union, they succeeded in hitting some Israeli aircraft though with less efficiency than expected given what must have been tens of thousands of shells fired. A Syrian gun crew is shown in action. (Albert Grandolini collection)

The S-75 SAM was initially deployed in 1957 to engage such targets as non-manoeuvring heavy bombers at up to 24,380m (80,000ft). The Dvina had a slant range of 8–29km (5–18mi). The missile possessed a 130kg (286lb) warhead detonated by proximity, contact, or command-signal fuses. The 2,250kg (5,000lb) missile had two-stages with the first of solid propellant and the second liquid. Motor burnout occurred in about 25 seconds with the missile flying at approximately Mach 3. The ground guidance system that could engage only one target at a time, although guiding up to three missiles simultaneously via radio with 65m (210ft) accuracy. The system usually relied upon the P-10 ('Spoon Rest') early warning radar with a range of 275km (170mi) while the 'Fan Song' acquisition radar had 65km (40mi) range. The later longer-range P-12 'Spoon Rest A' featured frequency-shifting and special capabilities to detect low-flying aircraft. A battery typically included six launchers arrayed around the radar and guidance control trailers. The launchers were usually 60–100m (200–330ft) apart and in revetments or earthen berms to protect against shell and bomb fragments. Egypt erected concrete walls against which they piled metres of sand suitable for protection from 500lb bomb blasts. At least at semi-permanent sites around airfields and cities the control vans were in concrete bunkers, some below ground. Ready reload of six missiles were usually on trucks nearby and transfer to the launcher could be performed in minutes.

Typical minimum engagement altitude of the S-75 was 915m (3,000ft), but upgrades reduced this by half. Since the missile was designed principally for operation in thinner air at high altitude, abrupt low altitude manoeuvres such as turn reversals and pitch-over/pull-ups in following the target could cause the missile to lose control or break up. Even lacking this the manoeuvring, after motor

Egyptian airstrikes on IDF positions in Sinai brought forth need for more effective and distributed ground defences. Israeli industry reworked an American system with twin 20mm cannon and placed it on several mounts. One such were captured Egyptian indigenous Al-Walid armoured personnel carriers as shown here. (IAF)

Egypt commonly employed the classical layout of the Soviet S-75 battery with the command trailer, fire-control radar, and equipment in the centre and the six missiles surrounding this. Camouflage netting would often be draped over these elements. This site has neatly built blast walls around the command centre and launchers, plus a lined dugout for reload trailers (towards the front of the image). (IAF)

burnout, bled energy and it might simply be unable to continue tracking the reflected radar signal. Visual sighting of the closing 'flying telephone pole' could give the targeted pilot time to evade. The Israelis had lost two fighter-bombers to the Dvina during the war for 15 missiles fired and the UARAF lost several aircraft to the missiles in friendly fire incidents.

In 1965–1966 the Americans had developed tactics and equipment to deal with North Vietnam's S-75s. These included aircraft to collect emission data and then to develop jamming equipment. Jammers, either selective or barrage, were placed internally on attack jets, as external pods, or on dedicated support aircraft. Also introduced were suitably tuned RWR to alert pilots of tracking by the Fan Song and so manoeuvre to break the automatic tracking. The air-launched AGM-45 Shrike anti-radiation missile (ARM) homed in on the guiding radar station. This had a range of 16km (10mi) – less than that of the SAMs. The Soviets responded with upgrades and ECCM capabilities. Improvised tactics included turning off the radar transmitter to cause the Shrike to 'go stupid.' However, this left any missile in flight unguided and, with warmup time and reacquisition, the enemy would likely have completed their strike and exited the area. An alternative was to cease transmitting but keep the unit powered up, reducing re-engagement time. The operators could also deflect the radar beam, and so potentially reengaging the target with a missile in flight. The missileers also altered the system to permit the missile to track on the jamming signal. They also fired in salvos.

The combination of EW and ARM was so effective that the Vietnamese and their Soviet advisors were finding that, by 1968, they were discharging more than 34 missiles for each kill. The attackers developed such tactics as flying with emission silence and hard manoeuvring beyond the capabilities of the missile to follow. This electronic combat swung back and forth between who held the advantage. After March 1968 the missile war subsided but the Soviets continued working upgrades to the S-75 answering deficiencies. These included improving performance against tactical aircraft, reducing susceptibility to jamming encountered to that time, and introducing an optical tracking capability. Americans had not faced these Desna and Volkhov versions.

The Vietnam SAM battle was an order-of-magnitude greater in scope than the Middle East experience. The latter combatants benefitted from weapon system developments that continued throughout the period of the War of Attrition. However, Israel had only a fraction of the resources of the USA. The largely level terrain allowed a very low altitude approach by attackers complicating SAM targeting and engagement. Israel's jamming and decoy methods were modest and effectiveness difficult to judge from accessible information. They used standoff aircraft with observers to give radio reports of missile launches. Chaff was not known to be used given the low-altitude ingress of the fighter-bombers and because support aircraft were too vulnerable.

The S-125 Pechora (export version Neva, SA-3 'Goa') was initially deployed in 1961 and had not seen combat. It used newer technology than the S-75 and was less susceptible to jamming. Typical slant range was 24–29km (15–18mi) at up to 12,190m (40,000ft). Most notable was performance at low to medium altitudes (100–5,000m/300–16,500ft) and against manoeuvring targets. It employed automatic radio command guidance with semi-active homing (on radar energy from the ground reflected off the target) for end-game engagement

The missile of the S-75 system was, along with the supporting radar, subject to the most change for improved variants. They all looked basically like this on the launcher. They were normally placed in revetments as seen here to help protect the equipment from nearby bomb blast fragments. (IDF)

with proximity fuse. Two missiles could be guided simultaneously against a single target. The 900kg (2,000lb) V-600 missile used solid propellant for both stages, flew around Mach 3, and had a 60kg (130lb) warhead. The V-601, introduced in 1970, was slightly larger with a 70kg (155lb) warhead. Powered flight was 24 seconds. The system employed the P-12 acquisition radar or P-15 Trail ('Flat Face' or 'Squat Eye') and 'Low Blow' radars. A battery typically consisted of the engagement radar, four dual-missile launchers, and trucks with additional missiles and reload gear. All equipment was relocatable on vehicles or towed trailers but was otherwise a semi-mobile system. Emplacement on a suitably hard and flat surface, with earthen berm protection, was common.

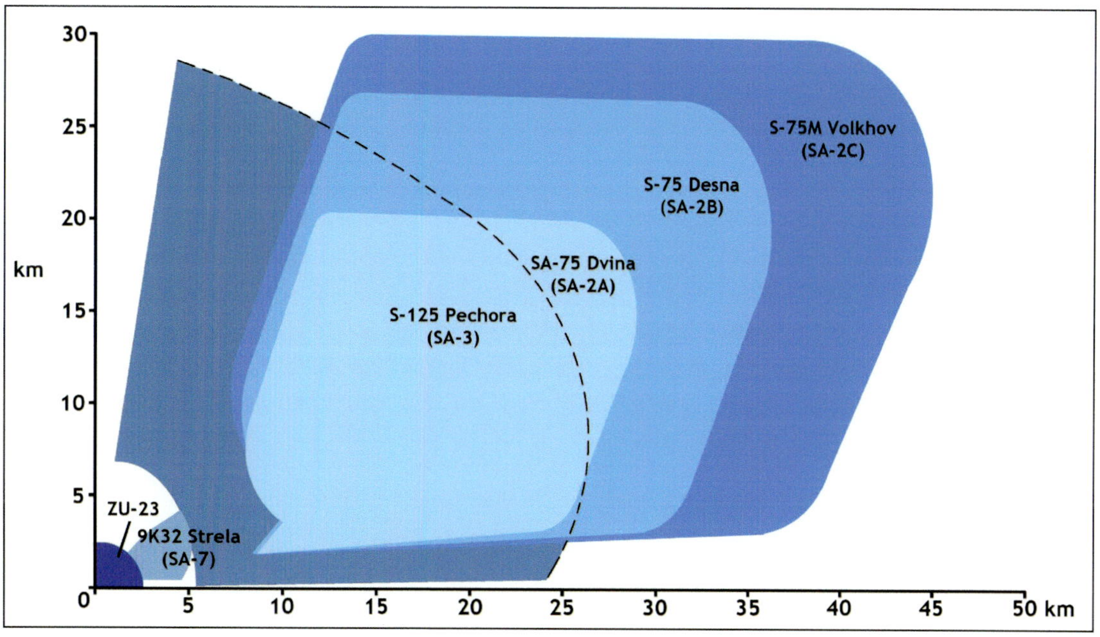

Typical engagement envelopes of the common Soviet air defence systems in theatre during the War of Attrition are depicted. The ZU-23 gun is typical of the small calibre weapons while larger weapons had expanded envelopes but similar profile. (Diagram by Tom Cooper)

The man-portable, shoulder-fired 9K32 Strela-2 (Arrow, SA-7 'Grail') dated from 1968 and engaged low-flying aircraft with an IR-homing missile. The entire system was 15kg (33lb), 1.4m (4.7ft) long, and with a missile possessing a 1.2kg (2.6lb) warhead. Flight was at 1,545kph (960mph), range 3.7km (2.3mi), and effective altitude 50–1,500m (160–4,900ft). The solid motor burned for less than 3 seconds and the missile self-destructed after 14–17 seconds flight time. The small warhead typically only damaged the target, and flares (not employed in the theatre) were effective in decoying the seekerhead. The launch tube was not reloadable in the field.

The MIM-23 Hawk system (formally HAWK for Homing All the Way Killer) had been in service since 1960. A battery normally included four towed radar units for search, track and guidance, a command trailer, six three-round launchers (fixed for firing), and three reload tractors of three missiles each. The full six launch units did not need to be employed. Hawk was a semi-active homing system with typical range of 1.9–25km (1.2–16mi) and engagement altitude of 60–11,000m (200–36,000ft). Each solid-

The Hawk missile was a fine system that was demonstrably more effective than the S-75. Israel had just a few batteries to defend high-value sites while relying heavily on interceptors to keep enemy air at bay. In October 1973 fighting it would demonstrate a 50-percent probability of kill. (Ofer Zidon collection)

fuel, single-stage missile weighed 585kg (1,290lb) with a 54kg (119lb) warhead. Powered flight was 26 seconds and reached Mach 2.4. While Hawk had good low-altitude engagement performance, the missile dived on very low targets which could then be lost in radar return ground clutter. Israel placed its batteries in fixed but revetted and camouflaged positions while also employing some dummies without emitters.

When deployed to Sinai, Israel's array of SAMs and AAA were concentrated around widely dispersed high-value areas. Hawk batteries, full or partial, were emplaced near the headquarters at Tasa, Refidim AB, El Arish, and other sites near vital assets like Umm Hashiba, or to control major air ingress points. Interceptors were relied upon to thin enemy attack formations before they reached such areas.

Table 12: Air Combat Systems, Fall 1973

System	Egypt	Syria	Israel	System
		Fighter-Bomber		
MiG-21	160	110	75	30 Shahak 4 Mirage IIIBJ 1 Mirage IIICJ(R) 40 Nesher
MiG-19	60	-	115	109 F-4E 6 RF-4E
MiG-17	200	120	181	162 A-4E/H/N 19 TA-4F/H/J
Su-7	130	45	25	Sa'ar
		Bomber		
Tu-16	18	-		
Il-28	30	-		
		Assault Helicopters		
	70	30	16	S-65
Mi-8	12	6	11	Super Frelon
Mi-6			37	Bell 205
		Combat Transport		
			2	C-130H
			22	Noratlas
not employed tactically			11	8 KC-97 (some in overhaul), 3 B-377
		Remotely Piloted Vehicle		
			8	Firebee 124I
			30	Chukar decoys
		Antiaircraft		
2K12 (launchers)	80 (300 missiles) or 10 battalions	60 or 15 battalions		
S-125 (launchers)	200 (1,400 missiles) or 64 battalions	20 (100 missiles) or 16 battalions (12 operational)	12 batteries (8 deployed), 72 launchers, 400 missiles	Hawk
S-75 (launchers)	420 (1,700 missiles) or 74 battalions	70 (200 missiles) 18 battalions (12 operational)		
Strela (missiles)	2,000 (128 platoons)	1,000 (64 platoons)		
ZSU-23-4	263	184		
ZU-23	450	258	219	40mm
20mm	400	255	770	20mm, various mounts
37mm	435-513	290	50+	37mm
S-60 (57mm)	488	294	?	S-60 57mm (captured)
85mm	180	140	?	85mm (captured)
100mm	362	170		
Some figures are best available information				

7

FIGHTING ACROSS THE JORDAN

Israel's counter-insurgency contest with Palestinian infiltrators and operations against national forces in Jordan grew in scale during 1968. One major incursion and multiple commando raids marked an increasingly violent campaign with airpower playing an ever-greater role.

LAND OF PURSUITS

Hundreds fedayeen crossed the Jordan River into the West Bank on their guerrilla operations. They crossed at night by wading or using crude rafts of tractor tyres or oil drums. Loaded down with gear, this was time-consuming and exposed the fedayeen to detection. Once across, it was impossible for the fedayeen to reach most of the towns and villages overnight. They had until dawn to avoid Israeli patrols or ambushes and usually went to ground in a cave where they would remain all day. After dusk they would march for several hours over rough terrain to reach their objective. They had to do this while avoiding IDF patrols and active efforts to intercept them.

The IDF and Border Police had to adjust and reorganise in meeting these incursions to intercept and eliminate the insurgents. These outfits adopted counter-insurgency (COIN) tactics to intercept the threat. The Border Police patrolled the western bank of the Jordan River while 612th Territorial Infantry Brigade operated around Hebron and in the Negev. These were largely passive operations. The 63rd (Parachute) Territorial Brigade (Jordan Valley), also called the Valley Brigade, was created from the headquarters of the reserve 80th Parachute Brigade on 3 November 1967 with battalions allocated from the active 35th Parachute Brigade and the reserve 55th Parachute Brigade augmented by troops from training establishments. Zahal personnel supplemented the civilians standing guard duty at their settlements, some Nahal.

Israel's fleet of Mystère IVAs continued to operate for a few years despite the French embargo on military materiel. They were valuable for the low-intensity conflict in the east but contributed over Suez as well. These 116 Squadron jets are armed-up for launch from Tel Nof AB supporting the Karameh incursion on 21 March 1968. The small weapons load of just two 250kg bombs is stark by comparison with the new A-4H. (Ra'anan Weiss collection)

An Alouette light helicopter is repositioning a small squad of soldiers as it did during the Jordan Valley pursuits of Palestinian infiltrators, 'jumping' the soldiers to intercept points, replenishing drinking water, and extracting casualties. The aircraft is fitted with a stretcher on the port landing skids and carries the Magen David Adom marking of a medivac craft, making one ponder its use in transporting armed personnel. (IAF)

Israeli operations intercepting these infiltrators were termed 'Badger.' The Valley Brigade soon achieved an elite status in these COIN operations. The teams initially performed their pursuit and engagement on foot, as demanded by the rugged terrain, and armed jeeps where possible. They assaulted the enemy with infantry tactics but this brought dismaying casualties. They began using helicopters in November 1967 and called in vehicles with heavy ordnance. If the guerrilla band was run to ground in thicket, jets with napalm bombs worked to eliminate them in 'Cricket' operations. Visual reconnaissance was also flown with light planes, called 'Crab' along the border and 'Grove' when into Jordan. Squadrons became familiar with specific areas to which they were assigned responsibility. These were comparatively rapid responses, airbases just a short flight away.

With helicopters available, once evidence was found that a squad had crossed the choppers lifted infantry teams into the vicinity to track and interdict. The rotorcraft remained in the area to perform airborne searches, reposition the team, or bring in reinforcements. With daytime temperatures occasionally exceeding 45°C (110°F), lifting in drinking water was also vital. The work

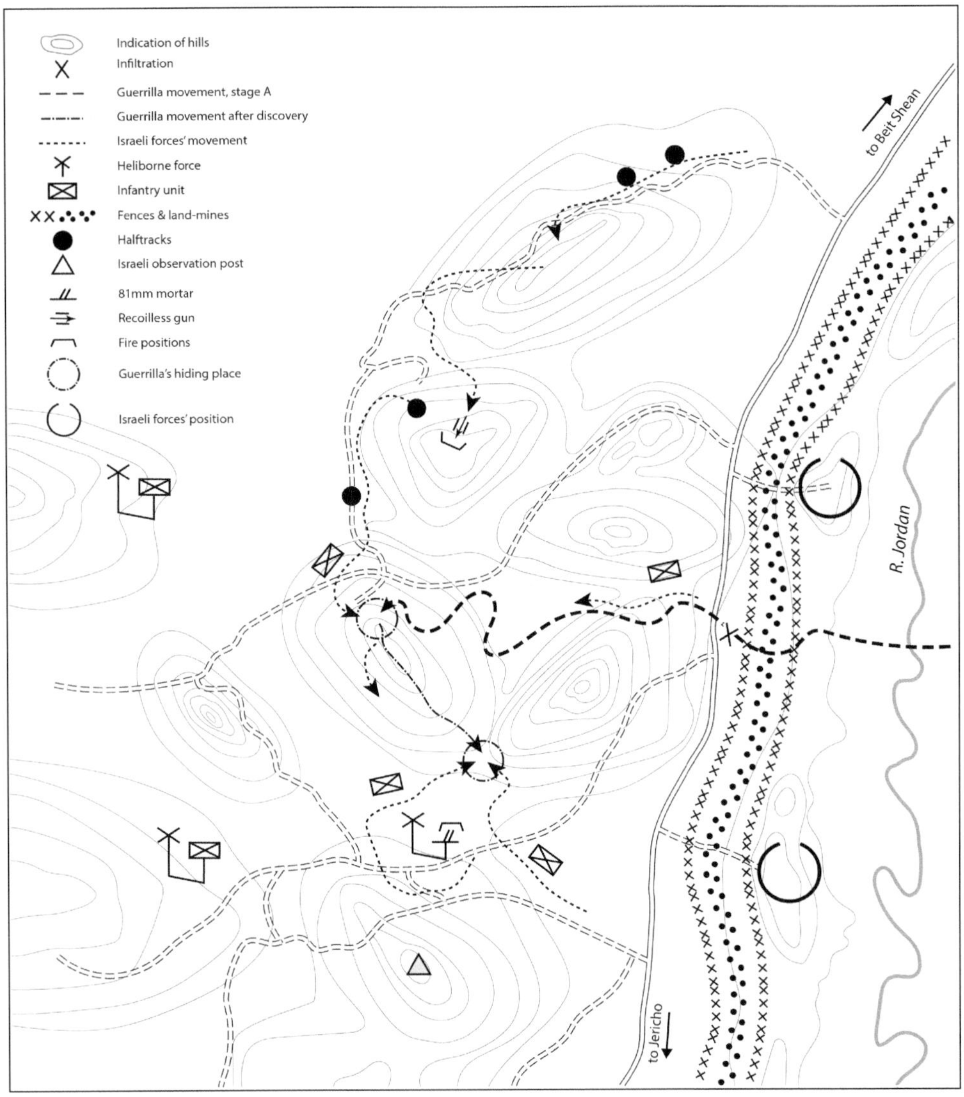

The map depicts one actual Jordan Valley infiltration and pursuit. The IDF resources brought to bear were considerable and the Palestinian team did not penetrate far into the West Bank before being neutralised. The use of helicopters to rapidly reposition forces in the final stage of the operation was surely critical to the success. (Map inspired by those appearing in books by Samuel Katz)

A group of Palestinian guerrillas march overland to their objectives equipped with a variety of weapons. Although lightly dressed for the hot climate, they lack boots and helmets as testament to their organisation's modest funding. The rugged, hilly terrain is typical of the West Bank landscape. (Albert Grandolini collection)

was initially performed by S-58s and Alouette IIs until Bell 205s had worked up to operational readiness. Many times door guns were used to pin down insurgents until the infantrymen arrived. Some work was done with the Hueys fitted with rocket pods and small bombs, but this was likely not common.[1] With caves serving as refuges and cache locations, the IDF made a point of locating and sealing caves in the region during 1969. Foliage along the river bank that helped to conceal the guerrillas or hide their passage was cut away or burned.

In reaching a town or village the infiltrators initially exploited personal and family links to create cells and bases. But soon the men sent were strangers. The inhabitants often regarded them with suspicion and were not reassured by occasional tactless behaviour and lack of discipline. They could be easily detected by Israeli civilian security service personnel who penetrated the organisations. For every fedayeen captured, denunciation or interrogation led to another 40 being rounded up. The fedayeen groups were not strong enough to terrorise or coerce the population. While generally sheltered and fed, the locals in large part would not cooperate in making trouble. They justifiably feared Israeli enforcement actions that including deportations, home demolitions, curfews and restrictions on movement – these multiplying as fedayeen attacks increased.

During 1967 the fedayeen (mostly Fatah) concentrated upon sabotage, mining and sniping with the IDF recording 61 incidents between September and December. It sparked a three-month Israeli security operation using captured Jordanian police files and records as well as their own intelligence information. This successfully disrupted fedayeen attempts to create a cohesive network and the insurgency was broken. The COIN operations were also increasingly successful in intercepting the fedayeen before they could push deep into the occupied territory. In combination this meant that, by November 1967, most of the fedayeen who crossed the Jordan were killed or captured. By the end of the year the Israelis claimed to have killed about 200 armed guerrillas and to have captured around 1,000.[2] In December they arrested 54 agents in the West Bank.

The destruction of their West Bank networks shaped a fedayeen strategy of striking across the Jordan in a terror campaign which continued until September 1970, vigorously opposed by the IDF. Initially infiltrating in groups of 40–50, Israeli COIN soon forced the guerrillas to operate in smaller groups. IDF figures showed 33 incidents on the West Bank in 1968 and 896 in the Jordan Valley, the latter including Jordanian and Iraqi artillery and mortar fire both to cover fedayeen crossings and as retribution for Israeli retaliatory raids.

It was a bitter and exhausting contest with the Israelis recording 5,840 hostile acts emanating from Jordan that saw 141 Israelis killed and 800 injured.[3] Eighteen months and 140 pursuits were required to largely quell the threat. Just in July 1968 the IDF fought 98 engagements against guerrillas inside the occupied territories and suffered depressing casualties as a result. By 1969 the effectiveness of the COIN operations had grown to where infiltrators were suffering 90 percent killed or captured – hundreds of fighters. About 1,000 Palestinian fighters were killed in the bloody period and many others found themselves in Israeli prisons.[4]

Given the great number of incidents, executing retaliatory strikes for each became impractical. Israel soon adopted passive methods. Much of the border was eventually lined with concertina wire, a pair of parallel electrified fences, and minefields, supported by a dozen outposts, patrols, and vegetation clearing. Some gaps were left in these barriers to channel enemy movement. Roads were cut where necessary and there was a swept path of soft earth in which footprints could be clearly discerned.

DUELS

Aside from guerrillas, the dozens of Jordanian tank and artillery shelling incidents were reaching intolerable levels. With the IDF not equipped to respond with sufficient or accurate counter-battery fire the air force was often called in. Heavy Jordanian shelling began on 12 February 1968. The entire frontier was aflame with artillery exchanges during 14–15 February, the IDF adding tank fire and bombing. This last was the first Israeli airstrikes on the front since November, hitting Jordanian batteries and other military posts on the border. Iraqis began participating on 1–2 December 1968 to which the IDF responded with its own shelling. Airstrikes were again resorted to with hits on 4 December killing eight and wounded 14 Iraqis along with considerable equipment loss, but losing an aircraft and pilot fatally injured by civilians. Much of the Arab action may have been without explicit instructions from Amman. However, the sporadic shelling of Israeli towns and IDF elements across the river, disrupting the lives of inhabitants, raised ire to breaking.

The contest continued intermittently until the IAF was flying frequent missions to the east. They also struck radar that served to warn of strikes even in Egypt, particularly a station in the north at Ajloun and in the south in the Moab Mountains.

Zahal engaged in many dozens of pursuits and firefights with Palestinian irregulars on both sides of the Jordan River. These came to be supported by air power, especially helicopters in observation and repositioning of squads. The Bell 205, with its turbine engine and generous interior volume accessed via twin sliding doors, was a great boon for special forces. These 'Hueys' have alighted in the Jordan Valley in support of a mission which has yielded two dead infiltrators. (IAF)

With their air forces initially deficient and ground combat limited, the Arab combatants grew heavily reliant on artillery. Shelling hitting Israeli civilians in the north and east, plus Egyptian fire in the south, became a common target for the IAF given the IDF's meagre counter-battery fire capabilities. Syrian gunners are seen in action during 1970. (Albert Grandolini collection)

Towed artillery did not have a large role in IDF doctrine, preferring SPGs that could advance with the tanks. However, largely staffed with reservists, the Artillery Corps was reasonably equipped to include this French Ubusier Modèle 50 155mm howitzer. Israel manufactured the ammunition for this and most other weapons it operated. (Albert Grandolini collection)

Jordanian AAA was more effective than those in other countries countering the IAF, the Israelis losing more aircraft there through 1970 than on other fronts. Jordan favoured Western armaments like this Bofors L/60 40mm gun and this may have been one factor in their success. (Albert Grandolini collection)

They eventually hit national infrastructure to dissuade the Jordanians from ceasefire violations. Leaflet drops and overflights of Amman for intimidation were also performed. Air action extended south to the Arava in early 1969. The French-manufactured jets came to be favoured on the front given an American proclamation that warplanes it supplied were not to be employed against the moderate kingdom. Later they wanted to restrain use of the aircraft while mediation efforts were under way with Egypt. Such Israeli compliance did not last long given the modest fleet size and operational demands.

Israeli shelling and bombing grew to an intolerable level in the Jordan Valley. This included hitting Jordan's very important East Ghor irrigation canal that was key to local agriculture and income. From first being struck by shells on 11 April 1968 it was repeatedly damaged through late summer 1969 by bombs and demolition charges planted by commandos. These rendered it inoperable and inflicting considerable agricultural losses. Most of the valley's 350,000 residents fled eastward and King Hussein eventually withdrew his forces as well. The PLO filled the void and intensified its campaign. The area became a virtual free-fire zone with the Israelis shelling and bombing to contain the guerrillas. As part of an American-sponsored ceasefire arrangement, Hussein agreed to remove fedayeen elements but proved powerless to do so.

The months into 1968 had visited on Israel's east an increasing and intolerable number of shelling and guerrilla incidents with casualties demanding a response. A particularly grievous incident drove the IDF to greater counteraction, although long contemplated. On 18 March 1968 a school bus ran up on a mine near Eilat killing two adults and injuring 10 children. Three days later the IDF turned its attention to the town of Karameh 3km (2mi) across the river. The 20,000 inhabitants had mostly emptied as armed militants took over. The objective was to destroy Fatah facilities in and around the town where Yasser Arafat had made his forward headquarters.[5]

BATTLE OF KARAMEH

Israeli intelligence estimated 900–2,000 opposition personnel were in Karameh. The IDF deployed between 1,000 and 1,500 personnel, including called-up reservists, making up roughly a division-size Central Command force. This included elements of the 7th Armoured Brigade (33 tanks), the 35th Parachute Brigade (800 paratroopers riding in halftracks), and a tank battalion on the 80th Armoured Brigade (13 M-51s, 3 Centurions, 9 AML-90s, and three SS-11 anti-tank missile teams with 12 launchers). All had engineering platoons, mobile command elements, and some mechanised infantry. More than 150 halftracks and other vehicles were employed. Three artillery battalions operated from the west bank.

The Jordanians became aware of Zahal preparations and the size of the force made them concerned Israel intended to seize a large area as an exclusion zone protecting the border and serving as bargaining leverage, if not march on Amman itself. They responded with their own deployment of thousands of men. This was a well-rounded force with infantry, artillery, and armour battalions made up of the area's 1st Brigade. Three infantry battalions covered the sector with a Guards battalion in reserve, plus a tank battalion from an armoured brigade based at Al-Salt. They were still short of heavy weapons but fielded around 50 Patton and Centurion tanks, 88 25-pounder guns in 11 batteries, and two reconnaissance regiments with Saladin armoured cars.

The IAF established a command post across the river from the Karameh battle, with a Noratlas communications relay aircraft overhead, to direct the air contribution to the 21 March 1968 infiltration. Brigadier General 'Beni' Peled (standing with handset to ear) leads the operation. He was then head of Air Department at headquarters and effective deputy air force commander. (IAF)

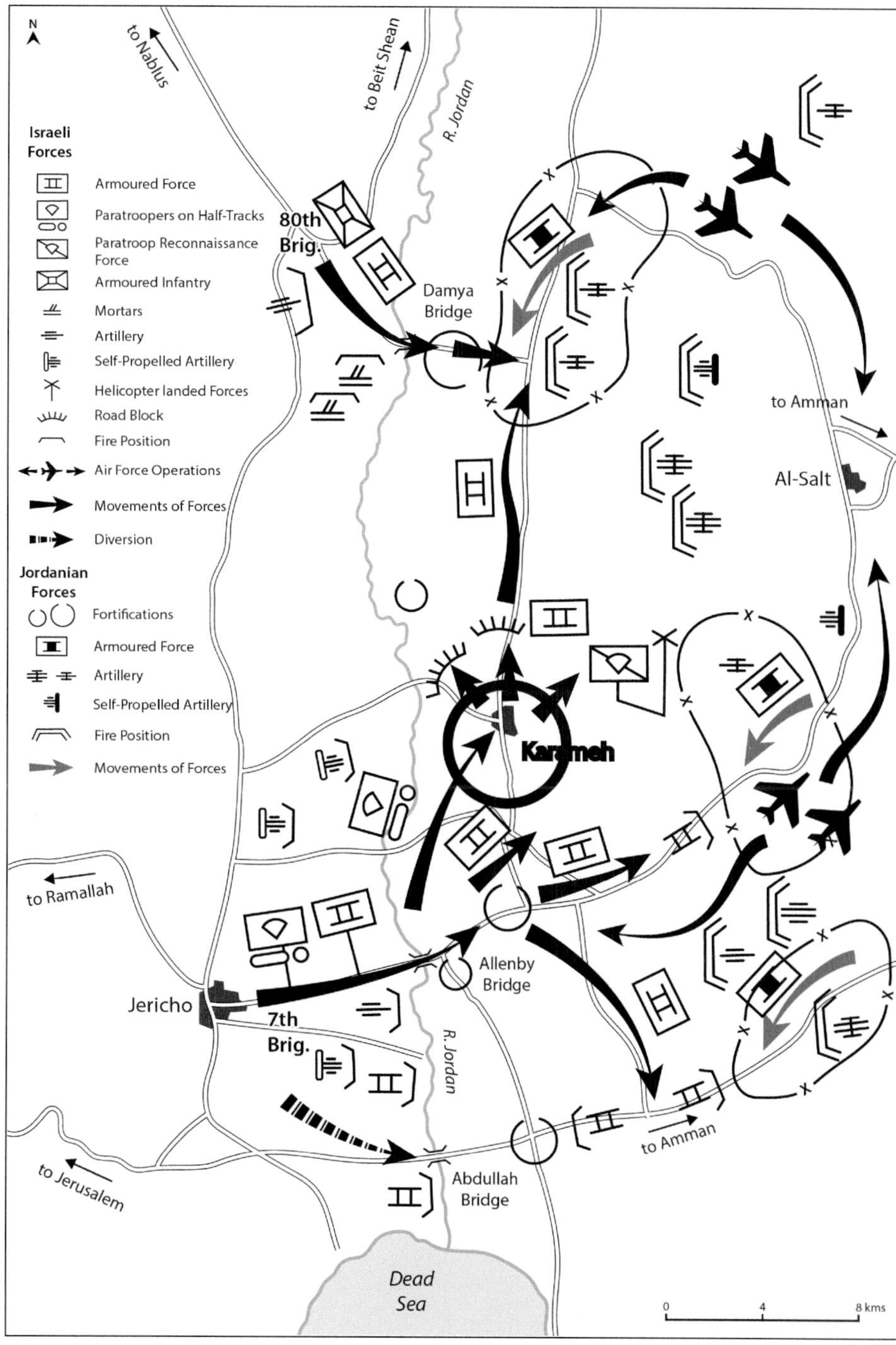

The Israeli incursion across the Jordan to eliminate the Palestinian enclave in Karameh involved crossing the Jordan River at two points, protecting the flanks of the main force, and landing paratroops to block the escape of militant to the east, as depicted on this map. A sizable Jordanian Army force was arrayed to greet the invaders who assumed these elements would not interfere. As is typical, the IDF plan 'did not survive the first engagement with the enemy.'

Aware of the Jordanian dispositions, the IAF dropped leaflets announcing that the IDF had no intentions to engage the Jordanians. Israel assumed they would not interfere and likely beat-feet to Amman. These forces held a geographic advantages and Jordanian troops were considered the best in the region. Israel enjoyed air superiority.

The operation did not go as planned, with approximately 33 Zahal personnel killed and 161 injured. Many vehicles returning were damaged and some under tow, with 27 of the 33 tanks 7th Armoured had sent across being hit. The IDF also had to leave three of their dead; something they worked hard never to do. Perhaps 156 Fatah fighters had been killed and almost 400 wounded, with 141 captured and infrastructure destroyed. Still, they were not as badly harmed as hoped. The Jordanians admitted 207 casualties, including 40 killed, with 25 armoured fighting vehicles damaged or destroyed, while Israeli sources give a figure of 334 including 84 dead with 30 tanks knocked out. Israel also held 12 Jordanian servicemen as POWs.[6] Although relatively successful, the results arguably did not justify the Israeli loss of life and equipment. The MoD put the best face on the disappointing operation. The Central Command chief, Major General Uzi Narkiss, retired shortly afterwards.

On the same day as the Karameh operation the IDF moved to eliminate irregulars from an area south of the Dead Sea near Safi. Helicopters brought in commandos while armour forded the river and the air force was overhead. They crushed the Jordanian and Palestinian opposition. The operation counted 20 fedayeen killed and 27 captured, plus around 20 Jordanian policeman and soldiers killed, and facilities razed. Saudi troops in the area, that aided the guerrillas, were also engaged. The IDF suffered no fatalities. Israel then occupied the site for three months, building a road to the crossing point. From this base patrols and surveillance outposts worked to keep the area cleansed of Fatah. After pacification, and with secret agreement from Hussein, Israel withdrew. The region was 'recaptured' in a well-publicised Jordanian armoured assault.[7] However, the Israelis returned twice more in the coming two years (see Volume 3, Chapter 2).

ASCENDANCE

The world community was nearly unanimous in condemning what was judged an excessive ceasefire violation. Jordan took heart at the good performance of its army at Karameh. They gained new confidence that it could defend the nation from Israeli aggression. The captured vehicles and equipment were displayed in Amman and photos of King Hussein atop a burnt Centurion were widely circulated, gaining him and Jordan some added measure of respect in the Arab world. Ignoring the Jordanian contribution, the PLO painted the battle as *their* victory, having 'repulsed' the previously 'invincible' Israel Army. This gained Fatah and Arafat added measures of favour in Arab centres. Arafat became the face of Palestinian resistance both in the Middle East and to the world.[8] His status among the Arab population rivalling that of Nasser. Money and training resources were offered and volunteers swelled Fatah ranks in Jordan. There were fund-raising drives throughout the Arab world while the oil-rich states, in addition to providing subsidies, also taxed the salaries of the Palestinian workers in their countries to aid the cause. The militant groups became bolder militarily but also took on more trappings of a government-in-exile. In the face of this heightened popularity Hussein was less inclined to confront the arrogant Palestinian irregulars. He tried to bring them under control of his army but the Palestinians would have none of it.

THE IDF IN TROUBLE

The 'police action' began at dawn, 0535, on 21 March, as the largest cross-border operation by the IDF short of war. Without artillery preparation, the IDF launched simultaneous assaults upon the three local bridges. Three tank platoons remained on the west bank to provide flat-trajectory covering fire. The intent was to isolate Karameh on three sides while the main force assaulted the town.

The 7th Armoured Brigade under Colonel Shmuel Gonen sent an armoured force with Centurion tanks and paratroopers in halftracks across the Allenby Bridge and a Bailey bridge engineers erected to avoid bottlenecks. They were to drive on the town while also isolating it from south and east. To the north the 80th sent their teams crossed the Damiya Bridge (also known as Adam) while throwing across another Bailey. They were to ensure local Jordanian armour did not drive south and interfere. The bridges had not been wired for demolition and the Jordanian defenders put up only light resistance before withdrawing. An approach to the King Abdullah Bridge (also known as King Hussein), south of the Allenby, was either a feint or abandoned after taking effective fire from the east bank.[9]

Israeli halftracks and AML-90s advance into Jordan on 21 March 1968 in an effort to suppress the Palestinian resistance centre at Karameh. Also supported by tanks and paratroopers, the IDF expected Jordanian forces to offer little resistance and to quickly crush the irregulars. (Albert Grandolini collection)

The spearhead 7th Armoured made reasonable progress towards Karameh until one battalion group was delayed after blundering into a flooded banana plantation. Extricating themselves, they were able to block the highway south of the town but spent the rest of the day under heavy Jordanian fire. Regardless, the battalion later repelled an armoured counterattack. The eastern blocking force also reached their station and then engaged in a long-range duel with Jordanian armour in which they claimed 15 tanks hit. However, the forward element missed a landmark and advanced too far. This cost them two tanks, including the battalion commander's vehicle, plus two halftracks with the forward command post and artillery liaison. Three dead were left behind in the burning Centurions under heavy fire. This force succeeded in repelling an armoured counterattack in the early afternoon by a battalion of the 60th Armoured Brigade. They claimed up to eight tanks and jeeps mounting recoilless rifles. At discouraging cost the armoured advances had prevent the Jordanians from interfering with the clearing of Karameh while the Jordanians felt they had prevented the Israelis from seizing territory or advancing on Amman.

Colonel Rafael Eitan's 35th Parachute Brigade, reinforced with a tank battalion, crossed on the Bailey bridge beside the Damiya. The intent was for them to go off-road to the south and approach the company of Jordanians in a fortified block from the rear. However, a dozen armoured vehicles became bogged down in the soft ground. Another element found a suitable route and executed the flanking assault that succeeded in expelling the Jordanians. They then took fire from enemy tanks that hit several vehicles before being silenced.

The foggy morning delayed by 15–20 minutes the deployment of an airborne blocking force to land east of the town. This was the paratroop sayeret company landed via 10 S-58 and two Super Frelon helicopters (which also brought in jeeps). Despite the delay the rest of the attack had proceeded on schedule. This included a leaflet drop by Mystères that alerted defenders of the coming attack. Deposited at the landing zone, the 70 paratroopers had to proceed on foot to their designated positions. Their late arrival allowed much of the forewarned Palestinians to escape Karameh and take up positions where they slowed the paratroopers and then engaged them in a deadly firefight.

About 200–300 fedayeen were left in the town, consisting mostly of Fatah but with some PFLP elements and a few other groups. Colonel Daniel Matt's 80th Parachute Brigade, with a battalion each of paratroopers and Nahal in halftracks accompanied by tanks, reached Karameh at 0700. Three Pattons met the force and in the ensuing exchange an IDF tank and two Pattons were hit, the third Jordanian vehicle abandoned. The urban environment offset the Israelis' superior training and the fedayeen resisted stubbornly. A particular problem was clearing a system of tunnels, the defenders expelled using smoke grenades. A force of six Jordanian tanks moved towards the town at 0900 but were hit by air strikes. Some 150

The Sikorsky S-58 (or H-34) had seen the IDF through the Six-Day War as the principal assault helicopter. It continued for another year in the role, especially casevac, specops, and repositioning personnel during the pursuit of Palestinian infiltrators from across the Jordan River. Here a 124 Squadron machine is taking casualties from the Karameh fighting. (IAF)

Jordanian 25-pounder guns are shown in action during the Karameh incursion of 21 March 1968. The Jordanian Army were widely regarded to be the best trained Arab force in the region and gave the IDF more trouble than they had bargained for during the day-long action. (Albert Grandolini collection)

individuals were rounded up in the house-by-house search and the questioned in an effort to identify the fighters. The town was not cleared until late morning.

Throughout the day more vehicles became bogged down and efforts made to extract them. In some cases this required a covering force that also took fire and losses. A persistent impediment was Jordanian artillery fire from the foothills overlooking the area, undaunted by Israeli counter-battery fire. Attempts at bombing them was also fruitless as they guns were well camouflaged and simply ceased firing when the approaching jets were spotted. The AAA that had claimed an Ouragan was cause to operate at higher altitude that limited attacks to bombs instead of rockets and napalm, and so affected accuracy and effectiveness. Still, dozens of (brief) sorties were flown with tons of ordnance delivered.

Zahal razed 175 buildings in Karameh that included demolishing most of the main street. Tonnes of seized munitions and enemy files were carried away. However, the PLO facilities were larger than anticipated. Central Command ordered a pullback at 1100 before the destruction had been completed. The return to the west bank was slowed by artillery fire that frustrated recovery of some vehicles, it was 2100 before the withdrawal was completed. Left behind were a jeep, a Dodge truck, two halftracks, a pair of AML-90s, and four Centurions. The penetration had been 12km (8mi) deep and 30km (19mi) in breadth.

King Hussein, Major General Sherif Nasser bin Jameel (civilian attire) and other military personnel examine one of the burned-out Centurion tanks left behind by the IDF in Jordan during the Karameh operation. Two of the four abandoned Centurions had caught fire and contained three servicemen whose remains could not be recovered. These, along with other vehicles and equipment, were displayed in Amman for the public to marvel at. (Albert Grandolini collection)

There were so many recruits flocking to the guerrilla bands, not all of them Palestinian, that waiting lists had to be drawn up. From 3,500 fedayeen, including 300 professional fighters, in March 1968, Israeli intelligence put fedayeen strength in Jordan, Syria and Lebanon at 7,500 by the end of the year. This would rise steadily to an estimated 12,000 by mid-1969. A growing militia of poorly-armed part-time men was estimated to bring numbers to about 20,000 or more. While the militias received some military and political training, they were usually employed collecting information, providing labour, obtaining supplies, raising money and as 'rent-a-crowds.' A program of youth training was instituted to grow a continuous stream of fighters. The professional fedayeen would serve a month-long tour at the front, mostly at the bases, then be rested for a month. Arafat said that Fatah's annual budget was then more than $70 million.[10]

The Palestinian fighters had never been better equipped. Their arsenal included infantry weapons including the excellent Kalashnikov AK-47 assault rifle, grenades, heavy machine guns and rocket-propelled grenades (RPG), recoilless rifles, mortars, Katyusha rockets, and explosives. Some of the heavier weapons were vehicle-mounted. There was plenty of ammunition, transport and communications equipment. However, the vulnerability of telephone and radio communications meant commanders tended to send written instructions by courier, even within Jordan. The munitions came principally from the Eastern Bloc, China, and Cuba, bought by Syria and Egypt, and entering Jordan via Palestinian and Iraqi units near the Syrian border. Jordanian efforts to control this flow proved wholly ineffective.

On 2 April 1969 Arafat took another step to dominance of the Palestinians when he created the Palestine Armed Struggle Command (PASC) nominally to direct strategy and coordinate operations. Its influence was great because it also controlled supplies of money and weapons favouring the larger organisations. However, neither the PFLP nor the PDLFP were members and relations within the organisation saw considerable friction between the members and their sponsors. A PLO delegation was admitted as observers to Arab summits and the oil-rich Saudis, Kuwaitis and Libyans agreed to raise their PLO annual subsidy from $90–100 million, agreed to in 1967, to $263 million. However, rivalries between the militant organisations undermined the PASC authority and acrimony grew to the point of faction leaders being targeted for assassination. This weakened the movement and made it vulnerable to suppression by Arab national forces.

RAMPING UP THE PRESSURE

Under relentless pressure from Zahal, the guerrillas had to move their bases east into the foothills along the eastern side of the Jordan Valley. They established 50 such bases along with a dozen field hospitals. The added distance meant an addition day/night for an infiltration team to reach inhabited areas. This left them more vulnerable to potential intercept. Continued attacks brought swift and harsh Israeli retaliation during cross-border 'Buffer' operations, declaring they reserved the right of 'hot pursuit' to cross any frontier. One of the guerrillas' major bases, at Al-Salt, was bombed by the IAF on 4 August 1968. Fatah then had to disperse to avoid becoming targets of air attack.

While raids by Fatah, augmented by a few by Saiqa, continued during 1968, their casualties were heavy with little apparent effect. For the fedayeen the effort of trying to reach the towns and villages of the West Bank was becoming a matter of diminishing returns. Zahal success drove the Palestinians to crossing the Dead Sea or further south to the Arava wadis. A favourite target was mining, mortaring, and ambushing traffic on the lonely road to Eilat. Israeli civil infrastructure and industry, plus the new oil pipeline from Eilat to Ashkelon, were also targeted.

During 1968 the IDF claimed to have killed or captured 2,650 fedayeen. Other Israeli figures indicate that between September 1968 and March 1969 there were 487 terrorist incidents; 189 from Jordan, and 123 from the Gaza Strip but only 29 originating on the West Bank. The Palestinians claimed, unrealistically, to have staged 1,000 incidents inflicting 900 casualties during 1968. They did evidently execute an average three operations per day with the IDF noting 112 incidents on the West Bank and 2,442 in the Jordan Valley. Zahal reported casualties in counter-insurgency operations between June 1967 and July 1969 as 40 while fedayeen dead during the same period was given as 461, with 119 during 1969.[11] In September 1969, Arafat confessed to the combat deaths of 700 of his men in the two years since the war.[12] By mid-1968 the IDF assessed fedayeen operations had become poorly planned and/or badly executed with attacks focussed less upon the security forces and more upon soft civilian targets. In 1969 these were reduced to just firefights across the Jordan, the odd hit-and-run raid to lay mines, and rocket attacks. By the end of that year Israeli COIN operations had largely neutralised the threat in and around the Jordan Valley. Israel claimed that during the year they detained 2,600 suspects including 100 Israeli Arabs and that 586 fedayeen were killed while 100 bazookas and mortars, 1,000 mines and 1,000 infantry weapons had been captured.

Embracing the theory that a good defence is a strong offense, the IDF sent patrols across the border regularly on 'Parasol' operations to monitor activity, lay mines, set ambushes, and snatch opposition leadership. These teams sometimes waited up to 36 hours to complete their mission. During 1969 and 1970 there were 28 operations with 17 sizable raids on PLO bases in Jordan by paratroopers.[13] Most or all were supported by helicopters. There were also attacks on Jordanian infrastructure as punishment for 'harbouring terrorists' and to induce Hussein to rein-in the irregulars. Hundreds of IDF patrols, small unit actions, fire events, and airstrikes were executed. The King became so concerned about these operations in August 1969 that he called on the Syrians for assistance. The IAF destroyed the Syrian artillery convoy as they moved south.[14] On 15 October Saudi forces in the south were bombed. Heavy strikes were again directed at the Iraqi force in Jordan on 26 November 1969. The IAF lost four fighter-bombers in combat on the front by the end of 1968 and six through April 1969. The IDF attributed this to the pilots fighting as in the war and so taking unnecessary risks. They were told to exercise more restraint and so tactics were adjusted.

The Bell 205, with its turbine engine and generous interior volume accessed via twin sliding doors, was a great benefit to IDF special forces, supporting many unique operations. The door hoist assisted in recovering downed aircrew. The Israelis added the door gun (FN MAG) and skid steps. This 124 Squadron machine has had the nose number smeared out by the censor who missed the same number on the tail boom. (Albert Grandolini collection)

One of the large-scale assaults occurred on the night of 1 December 1968 involving eight Bell 205s with four in reserve. The objective was the destruction of a pair of highway and railroad bridges on the main road from Amman to Aqaba. Three helicopters deposited paratroopers on the road to halt traffic. Two armed helicopters had to be called in to assist in this after the soldiers had been unable to stop the unexpectedly heavy flow of vehicles. The door guns managed to bring enough vehicles to a stop and created a satisfactory traffic jam, ensuring the safety of travellers while also delaying Jordanian Army interference. Three 205s then brought in 'sprinkler bomb' demolition charges under the helicopters, lowered into the proper position on the bridges. Two 250kg barrels carried by one helicopter were positioned on the railway bridge and a 500kg for each highway span positioned by individual choppers. Three minutes later the explosions dropped the structures and the paratroopers were airlifted out.

The highway bridges and irrigation canal had little military significance but they made clear to Hussein there was a steep price to pay for guerrillas launching attacks from Jordan. The King wished to halt the irritation but he had to walk a fine line between supporting the 'freedom fighters" aspirations, the appearance of continuing the struggle against the Jews, and seeking some unofficial accommodation with Israel to relieve the burden of war from his country. The PLO and its armed factions had grown very powerful and could threaten his rein and the nation's sovereignty. The armed forces had required time to recover from the war before effectively confronting the Palestinian threat, much less the IDF. The Palestinian personnel and those sympathetic risked splintering the army in any such suppression. Hussein's efforts to attract international assistance in seeking a solution were unsuccessful.

Israeli soldiers conducted many operations inside Jordan-proper in an effort to suppress the Palestinian terrorist scourge and compel the government to do likewise. No Arab soldier conducted similar operations inside Israel after 1948. These paratroopers are engaged in a firefight during the Karameh incursion. (IDF)

BIBLIOGRAPHY

Aboul-Enein, Youssef (ed.), *Reconstructing a Shattered Egyptian Army: War Minister General Mohammed Fawzi Memoirs, 1967-1971* (Annapolis, Maryland: Naval Institute Press, 2014)

Aloni, Shlomo and Avidror, Zvi, *Hammers, Israel's Long-Range Heavy Bomber Arm: The History of 69 Squadron* (Atglen, Pennsylvania: Schiffer Publishing, 2010)

Anon. INS *Dakar*, *Wikipedia*, <https://en.wikipedia.org/wiki/INS_Dakar>, accessed 13 July 2022

Avneri, Arieh, *War of Attrition* (Tel Aviv, Israel: Olive Books, 1972)

Bebars, Ahmed Abu, 'The Role of Electronic Warfare in the June 1967 War and the 1970 War', <www.group73historians.com> (Arabic), accessed 2021

Brugioni, Dino A., 'The Effects of Aerial and Satellite Imagery on the 1973 Yom Kippur War,' *Air Power History*, Fall 2004, pp. 4-13

Bull, Odd, *War and Peace in the Middle East, The Experiences and Views of a U.N. Observer* (London, England: Leo Cooper, 1976)

Central Intelligence Agency, 'The Middle East – An Arms Race', report CIA-RDP85T00875R001700070006-7, May 1974, Langley, Virginia

Cooper, Tom and Nicolle, David with Nordeen, Lon and Salti, Patricia, *ARAB MiGs, Volume 3 The June 1967 War* (Houston, Texas: Harpia Publishing, 2012)

Cooper, Tom and Nicolle, David with Nordeen, Lon, Salti, Patricia, and Smisek, Martin, *ARAB MiGs, Volume 4 Attrition War 1967-1973* (Houston, Texas: Harpia Publishing, 2013)

Cooper, Tom and Santana, Sergio, *Lebanese Civil War: Volume 1: Palestinian Diaspora, Syrian and Israeli Interventions, 1970-1978* (Warwick, England; Helion & Company, 2019)

van Creveld, Martin, Brower, Kenneth and Canby, Steven *Air Power and Maneuver Warfare* (Maxwell AFB, Alabama: Air University Press, July 1994)

Dayan, Moshe, *Moshe Dayan: Story of My Life* (New York, New York: Warner Books, 1977)

Dishon, Daniel (ed.), *Middle East Record, Volume Four 1968* (Jerusalem, Israel: Israel Universities Press, 1973); *Middle East Record, Volume Five 1969-1970 Parts One to Four* (Jerusalem, Israel: Israel Universities Press, 1977)

Dupuy, Trevor N., *Elusive Victory: The Arab-Israeli Wars 1947–1974* (Fairfax, Virginia: Hero Books, 1984); *Elusive Victory: The Arab-Israeli Wars 1947–1974* (London, England: Macdonald and Jane's, 1978)

Editors, 'Israel', *Armed Forces Journal International*, 111:2 (October 1973)

Epstein, Giora, *Hawkeye, The Enthralling Autobiography of the Top-Scoring Israeli Air Force Ace of Aces* (London, England: Grub Street, 2020)

El-Gamasy, Mohamed Abdel Ghani, *The October War* (Cairo, Egypt: The American University in Cairo Press, 1993)

Ginor, Isabella and Remez, Gideon, *The Soviet-Israeli War, 1967–1973, The USSR's Military Intervention in the Egyptian-Israeli Conflict* (Oxford, England: Oxford University Press, 2017)

Haloutz, Dani, *Eye to Eye* (Tel Aviv, Israel: ContentoNow, 2016)

Heikal, H. M., *The 30 Years War* (Cairo, Egypt: el-Ahram Publishing & Translation Centre, 1990) (Arabic)

Heikal, Mohamed, *The Road to Ramadan* (New York, New York: Ballantine Books, 1976)

INS *Dakar*, *Wikipedia*, <https://en.wikipedia.org/wiki/INS_Dakar>, accessed 13 July 2022

The Insight Team of the Sunday Times, *The Yom Kippur War* (New York, New York: ibook, 2002)

The Institute for Strategic Studies, *The Military Balance 1967* (London, England; The Institute for Strategic Studies, 1967); *The Military Balance 1968* (London, England; The Institute for Strategic Studies, 1968); *The Military Balance 1969* (London, England; The Institute for Strategic Studies, 1969); *The Military Balance 1970* (London, England; The Institute for Strategic Studies, 1970)

Johnston, Wm. Robert, 'Summary of Terrorist Attacks in Israel' <http://www.johnstonsarchive.net/terrorism/terrisraelsum.html>, accessed 24 June 2022; 'Chronology of terrorist Attacks in Israel' <http://www.johnstonsarchive.net/terrorism/terrisrael.html>, accessed 24 June 2022

Katz, Samuel M., *Follow Me!, A History of Israel's Military Elite* (London, England: Arms and Armour Press, 1989)

Korn, David, *Stalemate: The War of Attrition and Great Power Diplomacy in the Middle East, 1967–1970* (Boulder, Colorado: Westview Press, 1992)

Mommsen, Klaus, *60 Years Israeli Navy, Chel Ha'Yam Ha'Yisraeli* (Norderstedt, Germany: Books on Demand GmbH, 2011)

Morris, Benny, *Righteous Victims: A History of the Zionist-Arab Conflict, 1881–1999* (New York, New York; Alfred A. Knopf, 1999)

Nordeen, Lon, and Nicolle, David, *Phoenix Over the Nile, A History of Egyptian Air Power 1932–1994* (Washington, D.C.: Smithsonian Institution Press, 1996)

O'Ballance, Edgar, *The Electronic War in the Middle East 1968–70* (London, England: Faber and Faber Limited, 1974)

Olschner Clarence E., *The Air Superiority Battle in the Middle East, 1967–1973* (Pickle Partners Publishing, 2013, originally published in 1978, e-book)

Perlmutter, Amos, *Politics and the Military in Israel 1967–77* (London, England: Frank Cass and Company, 1978)

Roth, Asher, *The Air Force in the War of Attrition July 1967 - August 1970* (Tel Aviv, Israel: Ministry of Defense Publishing, November 1995) (Hebrew)

Rubinstein, Alvin Z., *Red Star on the Nile, The Soviet-Egyptian Influence Relationship Since the June War* (Princeton, New Jersey; Princeton University Press, 1977)

el-Sadat, Anwar, *In Search of Identity, An Autobiography* (Norwalk, Connecticut: The Easton Press, 1989)

Sakal, Emanuel, *Soldier in the Sinai, A General's Account of the Yom Kippur War* (Lexington, Kentucky: University Press of Kentucky, 2014)

Schiff, Ze'ev, *A History of the Israeli Army* (New York, New York: Macmillan Publishing, 1985); *Wings Over the Suez, The Story of the Israeli Air Corps* (Haifa, Israel: Shikmona Publishing Company, 1970) (Hebrew)

Sharon, Ariel and Chanoff, David, *Warrior, an Autobiography* (New York, New York: Simon & Schuster, 2005 e-book)

el Shazly, Saad, *The Crossing of the Suez* (San Francisco, California: American Mideast Research, 1980)

Spector, Iftach, *Loud and Clear, The Memoir of an Israeli Fighter Pilot* (Minneapolis, Minnesota: Zenith Press, 2009)

Spector, Iftach, *Victorious Losers, The Sources of Victory and Defeat*, draft book manuscript (September 2022)

Stockholm International Peace Research Institute (SIPRI) Arms Transfers Database, Trade Registers, https://armstrade.sipri.org/armstrade/page/trade_register.php, accessed 4 November 2022

Terrill, W. Andrew, 'The Nature and Value of Commando Operations During the Egyptian-Israeli War of Attrition', *Small Wars & Insurgencies*, 8:2 (1997), pp. 17-34

Transue, J. R., 'Assessment of the Weapons and Tactics Used in the October 1973 Middle East War', WSEG Report 249 (Arlington, Virginia; Weapon System Evaluation Group, October 1974)

Weizman, Ezer, *On Eagles' Wings* (New York, New York: Berkley Publishing, 1979)

Whetten, Lawrence L., *The Canal War: Four-Power Conflict in the Middle East* (London, England: The MIT Press, 1974)

Yaffe, Aaron, 'The War of Attrition in the "Land of Pursuits": The 1968–1970 War in the Jordan Valley', Ariel Center for Policy Research, <http://www.acpr.org.il/English/0907-YaffeE.pdf> accessed 5 April 2021

FURTHER READING

BOOKS

Almog, Ze'ev, *Flotilla 13, Israeli Navy Commandos in the Red Sea, 1967–1973* (Annapolis, Maryland: Naval Institute Press, 2010)

Bar-Siman-Tov, Yaacov, *The Israeli-Egyptian War of Attrition 1969–1970, A Case-Study of Limited Local War* (New York, New York: Columbia University Press, 1980)

Betser, Moshe and Rosenberg, Robert, *Secret Soldier, The Ture Life Story of Israel's Greatest Commando* (New York, New York: Atlantic Monthly Press, 1996)

Bowen, Jeremy, *Six Days: How the 1967 War Shaped the Middle East* (London, England: Simon & Schuster, 2003)

Bulloch, John, *The Making of a War: The Middle East from 1967 to 1973* (London, England: Longman Group, 1974)

Bulloch, John and Darwish, Adel, *Water Wars, Coming Conflicts in the Middle East* (London, England: Victor Gollancz, 1993)

Cobban, Helena, *The Palestine Liberation Organisation: People, Power and Politics* (Cambridge England: Cambridge University Press, 1984)

Cooper, Tom and Nicolle, David, *MiGs in the Middle East, Volume 2: Soviet-Designed Combat Aircraft in Egypt and Syria, 1963–1967* (Warwick, England: Helion & Company, 2021)

Cooper, Tom and Nicolle, David, *ARAB MiGs, Volume 2 Supersonic Fighters, 1958 - 1967* (Houston, Texas: Harpia Publishing, 2011)

Cooper, Tom and Salti, Patricia, *Hawker Hunter at War: Iraq and Jordan, 1958–1967* (Solihull, England: Helion & Company, 2016)

van Creveld, Martin, *Command in War* (London, England: Harvard University Press, 1985); *Moshe Dayan* (London, England: Weidenfeld & Nicolson, 2004)

Crosbie, Sylvia K., *France and Israel from Suez to the Six Day War* (Princeton, New Jersey: Princeton University Press, 1974)

Dishon, Daniel (ed.), *Middle East Record, Volume Three 1967* (Jerusalem, Israel: Israel Universities Press, 1971)

el-Edross, Syed Ali, *The Hashemite Arab Army 1908–1979, An Appreciation and Analysis of Military Operations* (Amman, Jordan: The Publishing Committee, 1980)

Eshel, David, *Chariots of the Desert, The Story if the Israeli Armoured Corps* (London, England: Brassey's Defence Publishers, 1989); *Daring to Win: Special Forces at War* (London, England: Arms and Armour, 1993)

Frisch, Hillel, *The Palestinian Military: Between Militia and Army* (London, England: Routledge, 2010)

Glassman, Jon D., *Arms for the Arabs: The Soviet Union and War in the Middle East* (Baltimore, Maryland: Johns Hopkins University Press, 1975)

Gunay, Murat, 'Armored Tip of the Spear, Build-Up During the War of Attrition, IDF Inventory Before Yom Kippur War 1973', <http:www.armored.bytehost17.com>, accessed 2021

The Institute for Strategic Studies, *Strategic Survey 1968* (London, England: The Institute for Strategic Studies, 1969); *Strategic Survey 1969* (London, England: The Institute for Strategic Studies, 1970)

de Lastapis, Jacques, *Military Powers Encyclopedia Volume 4: The League of Arab States (Irak, Jordan, Lebanon, Syria, PLO, Iran. Israel)* (Paris, France: Societie I^{3}C, 1989)

Luttwak, Edward and Dan Horowitz, *The Israeli Army* (London, England: Allen Lane, 1975)

Mangold, Peter, *Superpower Intervention in the Middle East* (London, England: Croom Helm, London, 1978)

Morris, Benny, *The Birth of the Palestinian Refugee Problem, 1947–1949* (Cambridge, England: Cambridge University Press, 1989)

Morse, Stan (ed.), *Modern Military Powers: Israel* (New York, New York: The Military Press, 1984)

Mutawi, Samir A., *Jordan in the 1967 War* (Cambridge, England: Cambridge University Press, 1997)

Norton, Bill, *Air War on the Edge, A History of the Israel Air Force and its Aircraft since 1947* (Hinckley, England: Midland Publishing, 2004)

von Pivka, Otto, *Armies of the Middle East* (Cambridge, England: Patrick Stephens, 1979)

Roth, Stephen J. (ed.), *The Impact of the Six-Day War: A Twenty-Year Assessment* (London, England: Macmillan Publishers, 1988)

Rubenstein, Murray and Goldman, Richard, *Shield of David, An Illustrated History of the Israeli Air Force* (Englewood Cliffs, New Jersey: Prentice-Hall, 1978); *The Israeli Air Force Story* (London, England: Book Club Associated, 1979)

Schiff, Ze'ev and Rothstein, Raphael, *Fedayeen, Guerrillas Against Israel* (New York, New York: David McKay Company, 1972)

el Shazly, Saad, *The Crossing of the Suez* (San Francisco, California: American Mideast Research, 1980)

Shimshoni, Jonathan, *Israel and Conventional Deterrence: Border Warfare from 1953 to 1970*, Cornell Studies in Security Affair (Ithaca, New York:, Cornell University Press, 1988)

Shirabi, Hisham, *Palestinian Guerrillas: Their Credibility and Effectiveness* (Beirut, Lebanon: Institute for Palestinian Studies, 1970)

Smisek, Martin, *Czechoslovak Arms Exports to the Middle East: Volume 1 Iran, Iraq and Israel 1948–1985* (Warwick, England; Helion & Company, 2021); *Czechoslovak Arms Exports to the Middle East Volume 3: Egypt 1948–1989* (Warwick, England; Helion & Company, 2022)

Stephens, Robert, *Nasser: A Political Biography* (London, England: Allen Lane, The Penguin Press, 1971)

Stockholm International Peace Research Institute, *SIPRI Year Book of World Armaments and Disarmament 1968/1969* (London, England: Gerald Duckworth, 1969)

Zertal, Idith and Eldar, Akiva, *Lords of the Land: The War Over Israel's Settlements in the Occupied Territories, 1967–2007* (New York, New York: Nation Books, 2007)

MONOGRAPHS

Nicolle, David and Cooper, Tom, *Arab MiG-19 and MiG-21 Units in Combat*, Combat Aircraft 44 (Oxford, England: Osprey Publishing, 2004)

Weiss, Ra'anan, *Israeli Air Force IAI Nesher 1971–1985*, Israeli Air Force Mini Photo Album No.3 (Kefar-Tavor, Israel: IsraDecal Publications, 2018)

Weiss, Ra'anan, and Aloni, Shlomo, *Dassault Mystère IV*, Aircraft of the Israeli Air Force 8 (Kefar-Tavor, Israel: IsraDecal Publications, 2010)

Zaloga, Steve J., *Red SAM: The SA-2 Guideline Antiaircraft Missile*, New Vanguard 134 (Oxford, United Kingdom: Osprey Publishing, 2007)

ARTICLES

Anon., *JTA Daily New Bulletin*, 14 August 1969, Jewish Telegraph Agency, New York, New York

Bentley, John, 'Inside Israel's Air Force', *Flight International*, 19 March 1970, pp. 426–429, 'Inside Israel's Air Force Part 2 – The Enemy We Face', *Flight International*, 23 April 1970, pp. 668–670

Aboul-Enein, Youssef, 'Egyptian General Abdel-Moneim Riad: The Creation of an Adaptive Military Thinker', *Infantry*, 93/2 (March 2004), pp. 12–15

Nicolle, David, 'Bearing the Brunt, Thirty Years of MiG-17 Service with the Egyptian & Syrian Air Forces', *Air Enthusiast*, 60 (November/December 1995), pp. 12–27

Yaffe, Aaron, 'The War of Attrition in the "Land of Pursuits": The 1968–1970 War in the Jordan Valley', Ariel Center for Policy Research, <http://www.acpr.org.il/English/0907-YaffeE.pdf> accessed 5 April 2021

LECTURES, LETTERS, PAPERS, REPORTS, AND THESIS

Bıçakcı, Ahmet Salih, 'Palestinian Liberation Organization: An In-Depth Analysis', DOI 10.13140/RG.2.2.10737.48484.

INTERNET

Ahmed Abu Bebars, 'The Role of Electronic Warfare in the June 1967 War and the 1970 War', Group 73historians.com

Feyrer, James, 'The 1967–75 Suez Canal Closure: Lessons for Trade and the Trade-Income Link', voxeu.org/article/1967–75-suez-canal-closure-lessons-trade

'Palestinian Journeys; Battle of al-Karama', https://www.paljourneys.org/en/timeline/highlight/165/battle-al-karama

'Sinking of the Eilat', steeljawscribe.com/2017/10/21/the-sinking-of-the-ins-eilat-50th-anniversary-of the first-surface-to-surface-engagement-with-ascms

ENDNOTES

Introduction

1. Nasser had come to power via a military *coup d'état* in 1952 (he was then a Lieutenant Colonel) and would come to hold near-totalitarian rule despite Egypt's forms of democracy, though Nasser limited it to a one-party system.
2. Egypt and Syria were combined administratively in 1958 as the United Arab Republic (UAR) that survived until Syria seceded in 1961. Egypt continued to identify itself as the UAR until 1971. In this account, it will be referred to variously as the UAR and Egypt.

Chapter 1

1. Photographs in the press of these men in the open behind barbed wire and guarded by IDF women soldiers incensed the Arab public.
2. Ariel Sharon and David Chanoff, *Warrior, an Autobiography* (New York, New York: Simon & Schuster, 2005), e-book, unpaginated (search for 'rough cotton').
3. The summary is based on an Egyptian assessment document that included those aircraft (fighters) lost during combat with the IDF in July 1967.
4. The literature is somewhat confused on the counting of S-75 batteries likely owing to the counting of un-deployed batteries and sites that may not yet have had an emplaced battery.
5. While some sources have it that the USSR delivered $2–3 billion worth of equipment through 1968, the USA's Central Intelligence Agency estimated Cairo received in 1967 the equivalent of $176 million of arms from the Soviet Union together with $25 million of tanks and jet trainers from Czechoslovakia, and $130 million the following year. See Table 6 (p. 16) and Appendix C of Central Intelligence Agency, 'The Middle East – An Arms Race', report CIA-RDP85T00875R001700070006-7, May 1974, Langley, Virginia. However, the quantity of equipment delivered would still suggest this estimate is low depending on how it is valued and the financial terms negotiated.
6. The stream of refugees from Gaza and the West Bank continued into Jordan after the war until that nation closed its border. The UN estimated that more than 100,000 post-1948 refugees had fled to the east bank with another 200,000 new refugees joining them. The extent of official or unofficial coercion by the IDF and other Israeli elements encouraging this migration has been argued for decades. While the Israelis said that these persons could return, and approximately 60 percent completed the necessary paperwork, both Jordanian and Israeli authorities made this so difficult that only 10 percent actually completed the journey back.
7. There has been a constant push-pull of referring to the armed Palestinian groups as terrorists, guerrillas, irregulars, militants, radicals, and freedom fighters. The forces targeted civilians and infrastructure much more frequently than military because of their comparative weakness for conventional warfare against a standing army with extensive defensive/offensive means. Given that they were seeking an insurgency and popular uprising, they could be considered guerrillas. However, many operations were blatant terrorism in the form of murder inspiring only revulsion and condemnation. It was a matter of perspective. This account will use the terms interchangeably based on the authors' assessment of the nature of the associated events.
8. The League of Arab States (*āmi'a ad-Duwal al-'Arabiyya*) is a long-standing association of Arab nations to coordinate policy and provide mutual assistance.
9. Source: Central Intelligence Agency, 'The Middle East – An Arms Race', report CIA-RDP85T00875R001700070006-7, May 1974, Langley, Virginia, Tables 5 and 6, pp. 15–16.
10. Stockholm International Peace Research Institute (SIPRI) Arms Transfers Database, Trade Registers, https://armstrade.sipri.org/armstrade/page/trade_register.php, accessed 4 November 2022. Much is period data with uncertainty as reflected. The table only reflects imports and not weapons manufactured in-country, this affecting particularly Israeli artillery systems.

Chapter 2

1. There are many dissimilar accounts of this affair. See for example Anwar el-Sadat, *In Search of Identity, An Autobiography* (Norwalk,

Connecticut: The Easton Press, 1989), pp. 192–194 describing Riadh and Fawzi finding Amer in pain at his home and having him transported to hospital where it was discovered he had attempted to poison himself. The later event in the villa where he was detained was investigated (the team including Amer's brother) and poison was strongly suspected. The field marshal's remains were buried hastily for the sake of dignity and to avoid a scene.

2. Some sources suggest the figure was only 70, some of whom were later re-instated.
3. Mohamed Heikal, *The Road to Ramadan* (New York, New York: Ballantine Books, 1976), pp. 41–41 and Mohamed Abdel Ghani El-Gamasy, *The October War* (Cairo, Egypt: The American University in Cairo Press, 1993), pp. 89–90. Heikal would eventually be named Minster of Information and National Guidance, and *Al-Ahram* was a mouthpiece for national policy.
4. These phases and their names evolved over time and did not come into focus all at once, although interpretation by historians and various translations of the Arabic words may well also play a role in the confusion. Likewise the timeline in which the phases were executed is also subject of variation in the literature.
5. Amos Perlmutter, *Politics and the Military in Israel 1967–77* (London, England: Frank Cass and Company, 1978), p. 45.
6. H. M. Heikal, *The 30 Years War* (Cairo, Egypt: el-Ahram Publishing & Translation Centre, 1990) (Arabic).
7. Tom Cooper and David Nicolle with Lon Nordeen and Patricia Salti, *ARAB MiGs, Volume 3 The June 1967 War* (Houston, Texas: Harpia Publishing, 2012), p. 53. This appears more credible than the claim in Edgar O'Ballance, *The Electronic War in the Middle East 1968–70* (London, England: Faber and Faber Limited, 1974), p. 72, that he was dismissed after the UARAF failed to suppress the heavy mortars that set Suez refineries ablaze on 24 October.
8. In the air force, only 21 percent of the personnel had a high school diploma, and only 9 percent in the army. Most had barely passed. Youssef Aboul-Enein (ed.), *Reconstructing a Shattered Egyptian Army*, War Minister General Mohammed Fawzi Memoirs, 1967–1971 (Annapolis, Maryland: Naval Institute Press, 2014), p. 30.
9. David Korn, *Stalemate: The War of Attrition and Great Power Diplomacy in the Middle East, 1967–1970* (Boulder, Colorado: Westview Press, 1992), pp. 93 and 295n36, from an interview with Major General Talaat Mosellem. This is misleading given that the air force had many more than 35 pilots and only a fraction of the population were of military age. However, it illustrates the problem.
10. Korn, *Stalemate*, p. 92.

Chapter 3

1. This summed to 68,572km² (26,476mi²) with 61,543km² (23,762mi²) from Egypt, 5,879km² (2,270mi²) from Jordan and 1,150km² (444mi²) from Syria. The new boundaries were actually shorter than pre-war – from 985km (612mi) to 650km (404mi) – the breakdown being 82 to 110km with Lebanon, 77 to 80km with Syria, 561 to 300km with Jordan, 206 to 160km with Egypt, and 59 to 0km with the Gaza Strip.
2. The western portion of Jerusalem had actually been only a quarter of the city and was subsumed in the 1949 post-war borders of Israel. It became the capital of the state from its inception and Israel considered the portion of the city under Jordanian rule to be occupied territory. Given the religious and regional sensitivities, and the potential role of the city's status in an eventual resolution to the conflict, most of the world's nation chose to establish their embassies in Tel Aviv. East Jerusalem was not truly annexed by Israel until a 1980 law declaring it Israel's 'eternal and indivisible' capital and extending civil law over the whole of the city. Most countries did not recognise this annexation.
3. Sharon and Chanoff, *Warrior* (search for 'various military schools' and 'managed to occupy'). In his roles as director of military training, Major General Sharon pushed to 'move various military schools from their old bases into Samaria' and 'within months I was able to transfer quite a number of them; the infantry school, the engineering school, the military police school, part of the artillery school, the main basic training school for new recruits, the paratrooper recruit school, and others.' And '... by 1968 I managed to occupy almost every single one of the old Jordanian military bases and police outposts outside of the cities.'
4. Dani Haloutz, *Eye to Eye* (Tel Aviv, Israel: ContentoNow, 2016), p. 48.
5. Israel spoke of going from four minutes for an Egyptian jet bomber flying from El Arish to the Tel Aviv area to 16 minutes, and smaller numbers for supersonic interceptors (without bombs and so not a significant threat). This assumed the aircraft was at maximum groundspeed passing over El Arish and flew directly to the Israeli city. Following the war these or Iraqi bombers, if based in Jordan or Syria, could still be over the city in minutes. From Refidim and Ophir, IAF aircraft were also that much closer to hitting major Egyptian cities.
6. Emergency-posting (EP) pilots occupied staff or training billets but maintained currency with an operational squadron with which they would fight in an emergency.
7. The military also permitted a ski resort to be established on the Mount Hermon in 1971.
8. Civilian population transfer into occupied territory violates the Geneva Convention that Israel ratified in 1951, and the government was advised of this. However, her lawyers came to argue various points in disagreement.
9. General Bull relinquished the post to at the end of July 1970 to Finnish General Ensio Sillasvuo.
10. Odd Bull, *War and Peace in the Middle East, The Experiences and Views of a U.N. Observer* (London, England: Leo Cooper, 1976), p. 153.
11. This marked only the fourth Arab League's summit since these began in 1964.
12. Many of the ministers in Prime Minister Levi Eshkol's cabinet insisted this was not formal acceptance.

Chapter 4

1. In 1966 21,250 ships sailed through the canal. O'Ballance, *The Electronic War in the Middle East*, p. 23. Fifteen commercial ships from eight nations had become stranded in the waterway by the closure, mostly in the Great Bitter Lake, on which skeleton crews remained. Efforts at negotiating a means of allow them to sail free could never be satisfactorily finalised with the parties. Becoming covered with sand, they earning the nickname The Yellow Fleet. Some of these vessels would be damaged and sunk over the next several years. When finally freed years later all but two had to be scrapped.
2. Forced to sail around Africa, crude oil en route to Europe from the Persian Gulf was delivered in ever-larger tankers to make the longer voyages cost-effective. The 'supertankers' eventually exceeded the width capacity of the canal. To service Mediterranean customers, Israel and Iran built an oil pipeline from Eilat to Ashkelon from whence the oil was again pumped to tankers. The Egyptians constructed a pipeline for similar purpose. Freight was also moved through the area, from coast to coast, to avoid the time

and expense of sailing around Africa. So, the significance of the Suez Canal closure dimmed over time.

3. Alvin Z. Rubinstein, *Red Star on the Nile, The Soviet-Egyptian Influence Relationship Since the June War* (Princeton, New Jersey; Princeton University Press, 1977), p. 164.
4. Klaus Mommsen, *60 Years Israeli Navy, Chel Ha'Yam Ha'Yisraeli* (Norderstedt, Germany: Books on Demand GmbH, 2011), p. 125. There are less well researched accounts having the Israeli MTBs attacked first and the destroyer coming to their rescue.
5. Editors, 'Israel', *Armed Forces Journal International*, 111:2 (October 1973), p. 51.
6. Along with the oil field the Israel Air Force also began operating the Hiller UH-12E4 helicopter (SU-AOP becoming 3302/4X-BHB), owned by an Italian firm, which communicated with the offshore facility. Operating the rig and exploiting the natural resources of occupied territory was of questionable legality. The Egyptians chose not to attack the facility and the Israelis, likewise, did not attack other Egyptian oil drilling operations at El Morgan, a few kilometres away. The importance of the oil production to the Israeli economy would grow over the next eight years. The oil was loaded onto tankers that unloaded at Eilat, the oil then pumped to Ashkelon, on the Mediterranean coast, via a newly-installed pipeline.
7. Korn, *Stalemate*, pp. 99-100.
8. In a 17 January 1970 article in the newspaper *Al Akhbar* Egypt claimed their frigate *Assyout* had detected and attacked *Dakar* on 23 January with depth charges just 3km (2mi) off Alexandria. This forced the boat to make an emergency dive and the *Assyout* lost track of her. They believed the submarine hit the ocean floor causing fatal damage. See INS *Dakar*, *Wikipedia*, <https://en.wikipedia.org/wiki/INS_Dakar>, accessed 13 July 2022. The Israelis dismissed the report as there was no rational reason for *Dakar* to be so close to the Egyptian coast. (The Egyptians speculate it was there to assassinate Nasser who was aboard a warship observing naval exercises.) Her last transmission was on the 25th and identified the boat's position as off Crete. After several search campaigns the *Dakar* was finally located in 1999 on the seabed between Crete and Cyprus. It had been crushed by rapid descent to excessive depth for reasons unknown, but an accident was the most likely scenario.
9. Soviet participation in this event is argued to the present day. Isabella Ginor and Gideon Remez, *The Soviet-Israeli War, 1967–1973, The USSR's Military Intervention in the Egyptian-Israeli Conflict* (Oxford, England: Oxford University Press, 2017), p. 32, quotes a Soviet naval officer saying that his team did all but press the button to fire the missiles. Elsewhere they relate other accounts of Soviet personnel aboard the boats given the Egyptian Navy's low state of readiness.
10. Given the extent of the damage inflicted, the possibility the cities were deliberately targeted as retribution cannot be dismissed, although poor gunnery is also likely to have played a role.
11. This was the first instance in modern times that Palestinian became a distinct regional and political entity.
12. Aboul-Enein, *Reconstructing a Shattered Egyptian Army*, p. 90.
13. Tom Cooper and Sergio Santana, *Lebanese Civil War: Volume 1: Palestinian Diaspora, Syrian and Israeli Interventions, 1970–1978* (Warwick, England; Helion & Company, 2019), p. 22 (Table 2), modified with multiple other sources.
14. By one counting the deaths amounted to less than five percent of Israel's national automobile accident fatalities, 529 in 1970 alone. Ze'ev Schiff, *A History of the Israeli Army* (New York, New York: Macmillan Publishing, 1985), p. 169 and Emanuel Sakal, *Soldier in the Sinai, A General's Account of the Yom Kippur War* (Lexington, Kentucky: University Press of Kentucky, 2014), p. 41. However, a civilian's murder by self-identified enemies is hardly an 'irritant' and the violence was an assault on national security that was bound only to increase without enforcement counteraction.
15. The table shows guerrilla/terrorist incidents inside Israel and the associated casualties (many civilians). This derives from two sources as indicated. Although the numbers differ, the table does indicate the scale and trend of the violence. There are obvious problems with the Johnston Archive numbers, such as no attacks in 1967 but 16 people killed. The data on the left are from Wm. Robert Johnston, 'Summary of Terrorist Attacks in Israel' <http://www.johnstonsarchive.net/terrorism/terrisraelsum.html>, accessed 24 June 2022 and Wm. Robert Johnston, 'Chronology of terrorist Attacks in Israel' <http://www.johnstonsarchive.net/terrorism/terrisrael.html>, accessed 24 June 2022. The numbers are principally those provided by the Israel Foreign Ministry while those killed in parenthesis are derived from a summary of individual incidents. The data on the right is from Daniel Dishon (ed.), *Middle East Record, Volume Four 1968* (Jerusalem, Israel: Israel Universities Press, 1973), p. 352, and Daniel Dishon (ed.), *Middle East Record, Volume Five 1969–1970 Parts One to Four* (Jerusalem, Israel: Israel Universities Press, 1977), p. 229, and also shown in context of all fronts in Volume 3, Appendix II. The numbers in parenthesis indicate the number of civilians included in the principal numbers. All are derived from IDF Spokesman reports.
16. The number derives from W. Andrew Terrill, 'The Nature and Value of Commando Operations During the Egyptian-Israeli War of Attrition', *Small Wars & Insurgencies*, Vol. 8 No 2, 1997, p. 21.

Chapter 5

1. Aboul-Enein, *Reconstructing a Shattered Egyptian Army*, p. 77.
2. Among these was a purported November 1969 incident in which a Su-7M suffered combat damage and was abandoned near the Gidi Pass, Sinai. The aircraft reportedly came down on its belly in soft, flat sand and so was recovered for examination. The account has not been publicised by Israelis, as have all the others.
3. A Heliopolis Gomhouria Mk.2 (Bücker Bü 181B Bestman) captured during the Six-Day War was operated by 100 Squadron for two years though likely only in ceremonies and demonstrations.
4. In December 1967 an Egyptian flight discovered a landing strip being constructed by the Israelis near Baluza, northwest Sinai. They immediately planned to bomb the site but Soviet advisors put a kibosh on the operation prompting the strike. Tom Cooper and David Nicolle with Lon Nordeen, Patricia Salti and Martin Smisek, *ARAB MiGs, Volume 4 Attrition War 1967-1973* (Houston, Texas: Harpia Publishing, 2013), pp. 54–55 and O'Ballance, *The Electronic War*, p. 73.
5. There had been a policy to permanently ground any pilot who had been captured by the Israelis, though this was at least partially set aside in time. Cooper, et al, *ARAB MiGs, Volume 4 Attrition War 1967-1973*, p. 46.
6. In Asher Roth, *The Air Force in the War of Attrition July 1967 - August 1970* (Tel Aviv, Israel: Ministry of Defense Publishing, November 1995) (Hebrew), Preface, Major General Herzl Bodinger mentions Vautour training flights particularly being curtailed owing to the lack of spares. Ze'ev Schiff, *Wings Over the Suez, The Story of the Israeli Air Corps* (Haifa, Israel: Shikmona

Publishing Company, 1970), p. 111, indicates that Mirages and Vautours were the most impacted.

7. The weapons pylons and guns were all deleted by 1972 and, it is assumed, the reserve 147 Squadron disappeared at that time or earlier. However, from immediately following the war the likelihood that the armed Magisters would be employed again in combat was remote.
8. The Mirage IIIS operated with the Atar 9B while the Israeli Mirage 5 used the Atar 9C. Sulzer Brothers would not have had the airframe details aside from, perhaps, interface fittings and attachments. It is doubtful the delivered incomplete drawings were of any significant value to Israeli aircraft programs.
9. Dassault actually produced just 42 percent of the Mirage directly, with some 50 other companies contributing. Thus, it is not surprising that parts of the Nesher were produced by firms other than Dassault and not likely as a means to remain covert.
10. This would have been in violation of third-party sales in the French contact without explicit consent.
11. The IAF had a shallow combat aircraft navigator tradition and the IAF commander told the first trainees to prove that the Phantom could be operated on most missions by the pilot alone. This was quickly shown to be impractical given design of the systems and the tremendous capabilities offered by the crew concept. Shlomo Aloni and Zvi Avidror, *Hammers, Israel's Long-Range Heavy Bomber Arm: The History of 69 Squadron* (Atglen, Pennsylvania: Schiffer Publishing, 2010), p. 106.
12. The deliveries were made by McDonnell Douglas flight test personnel at the request of the Defense Department for the sake of appearances (though the aircraft bore American national insignia). This caused a bit of disharmony among employees and some quit rather than participate in what appeared to be 'gun-running.'
13. Arieh Avneri, *War of Attrition* (Tel Aviv, Israel: Olive Books, 1972), p. 188.

Chapter 6

1. There is evidence the Soviets flew combat sorties as early as 1968, to include attacks in Sinai, as demonstration of the suitability of the aircraft and efficacy of tactics. See, for example, Ginor and Remez, *The Soviet-Israeli War*, p. 45.
2. Israel had insisted that their fighter pilots logged more flight hours than their Arab counterparts. Although this bears some logic given the IAF's higher operations tempo and combat on multiple fronts, the source of the numbers offered for their adversaries was never stated. They claimed about 200 hours per annum compared with an average 70 hours for Egyptian pilots. The latter number is contradicted by contemporary sources. Sources suggest that Israeli operational fighter pilots flew at least 288 hours pre-war compared with 120–150 for UARAF counterparts. O'Ballance, *The Electronic War in the Middle East*, p. 79, and Lon Nordeen, and David Nicolle, *Phoenix Over the Nile, A History of Egyptian Air Power 1932–1994* (Washington, D.C.: Smithsonian Institution Press, 1996), p. 226. Interviews and review of logs suggest as high as 200 hours for the UARAF while the IAF number appears high. Post-war hours reflected the Arab goal of improving performance. The Egyptians sought 240–288 hours annually but were logging as many as 500. See Nordeen and Nicolle, *Phoenix Over the Nile*, p. 226, Clarence E. Olschner, *The Air Superiority Battle in the Middle East, 1967–1973* (Pickle Partners Publishing, 2013, originally published in 1978, e-book), unpaginated (Chapter II under header 'Preparation of the Egyptian Air Force') and Cooper, et al, *ARAB MiGs, Volume 3*, p. 212. Fawzi spoke of a three-fold increase in flight hours, Aboul-Enein, *Reconstructing a Shattered Egyptian Army*, p. 107. One veteran IAF fighter pilot and squadron commander from the period offered an average 240 hours annually. (The year between summer 1969 and summer 1970 would likely have an unusually high value in this average given the scale of the fighting.) Flights in Soviet fighter-bombers seldom lasted more than 30 minutes whereas those in Western jets could be more than an hour depending upon mission and external tanks. So, the UARAF pilots likely logged more sorties.
3. The IAF had a legacy of aggressiveness fostered to some extent by organisational culture, and by the hazards of ongoing operations imbued young pilots with a sense of embracing danger. Consequently, reckless flying was typical and subject to relatively mild rebuke.
4. The Israelis altered the F-4's lowest fixed air-to-air engagement range from 300 to 250m (980 to 820ft) for firing based on an impression that pilots should be willing to close tighter on his adversary. Aloni and Avidror, *Hammers*, p. 106.
5. The Israeli Mirage squadrons fired 26 Shafrirs and four Matra R.530s during the war. Apart from a non-lethal Shafrir hit on an Iraqi Tu-16, the AAMs did not score. (The R.530 was retired soon after the war.) By contrast, it is fairly certain that three Egyptian MiG-21s and three Syrians scored kills with R-3S (two with cannon contributing), and a Mirage barely made it back to Israel with a badly mangled engine exhaust from a SyAAF R-3S hit.
6. Iftach Spector, *Loud and Clear, The Memoir of an Israeli Fighter Pilot* (Minneapolis, Minnesota: Zenith Press, 2009), pp. 216 and 239, describes championing adoption of the AIM-9D from the F-4Es to 101 Squadron Mirages. The air force already had a launcher adapted to the French pylon and agreed to test it on Major Spector's jets, to which the squadron installed an AIM-9D without authorisation and took it into combat with minimal testing and training. Spector scored a kill with it but another aircraft suffered a minor mishap. Yet, days later the other two Mirage units had the installation and weapons, and shot down more aircraft.
7. Iftach Spector, *Victorious Losers, The Sources of Victory and Defeat*, draft book manuscript (September 2022), Chapter 4 p. 9.
8. Cooper, et al, *ARAB MiGs Volume 4*, p. 76, gives the experience of six Egyptian pilots in one battle during early 1969 that together fired no fewer than 11 R-3Ss from 'favourable' positions with no hits.
9. When in late 1969 President Muammar Gaddafi had offered to acquire weapons for Egypt, Nasser encouraged him to seek Mirages. France insisted that the transaction was predicated on the aircraft not being transferred to Egypt or Syria. Gaddafi intentionally misled the French who were eager for the sale.
10. Saad el Shazly, *The Crossing of the Suez* (San Francisco, California: American Mideast Research, 1980), p. 196.
11. Martin van Creveld, Kenneth Brower and Steven Canby *Air Power and Maneuver Warfare* (Maxwell AFB, Alabama: Air University Press, July 1994), p. 170.
12. See Ahmed Abu Bebars, 'The Role of Electronic Warfare in the June 1967 War and the 1970 War,' <www.group73historians.com>, accessed 2021.
13. Lawrence L. Whetten, *The Canal War: Four-Power Conflict in the Middle East* (London, England: The MIT Press, 1974), p. 79. According to this author one goal of the Rabat summit in December 1969 was to seek funds to buy such equipment. Nasser also had pressed for EW systems during his June-July 1970 visit to

Moscow. Aboul-Enein, *Reconstructing a Shattered Egyptian Army*, p. 141. Saad el Shazly, *The Crossing of the Suez* (San Francisco, California: American Mideast Research, 1980), p. 175 relates that Sadat made the same appeal in May 1972.

14. Ginor and Remez, *The Soviet-Israeli War*, pp. 189–190 and Shazly, *The Crossing of the Suez*, pp. 83 and 166.
15. Fawzi credits the introduction of Soviet EW systems as July 1970 and Gamasy gives the August date for establishment of an Egyptian EW shop. Aboul-Enein, *Reconstructing a Shattered Egyptian Army*, p. 132 and El-Gamasy, *The October War*, p. 125.
16. J. R. Transue, 'Assessment of the Weapons and Tactics Used in the October 1973 Middle East War', WSEG Report 249 (Arlington, Virginia; Weapon System Evaluation Group, October 1974), p. 97, identifies the principal components of this system as American-supplied AN/ALT-6B and -27 jammers.
17. The Insight Team of the Sunday Times, *The Yom Kippur War* (New York, New York: ibook, 2002), p. 33, without attribution. However, the description of the capability suggests this was merely RWR for which the Americans provided AN/APR-36 and -37 units with the Phantoms or separately.
18. Dino A., Brugioni, 'The Effects of Aerial and Satellite Imagery on the 1973 Yom Kippur War,' *Air Power History*, Fall 2004, p. 9.

Chapter 7

1. Information from an Israeli researcher who also showed photos printed in a book on the history of 123 Squadron.
2. Benny Morris, *Righteous Victims: A History of the Zionist-Arab Conflict, 1881–1999* (New York, New York; Alfred A. Knopf, 1999), p. 366.
3. Moshe Dayan, *Moshe Dayan: Story of My Life* (New York, New York: Warner Books, 1977), p. 497. The figure includes artillery and mortar fire from Jordanian and Iraqi army positions.
4. Ezer Weizman, *On Eagles' Wings* (New York, New York: Berkley Publishing, 1979), p. 258.
5. The IDF had hoped to sweep up Arafat with other fedayeen or kill him if necessary. One of the captured Fatah members said at a news conference that Arafat had organised the resistance then left with his deputy to fight another day. Other account refuted that Arafat was even in the town at the time of the attack. Israel made targeted attempts on the life of the PLO leader, two detailed in Giora Epstein, *Hawkeye, The Enthralling Autobiography of the Top-Scoring Israeli Air Force Ace of Aces* (London, England: Grub Street, 2020), p. 70. The first was a 1968 strike, probably by Ouragans, on two automobiles travelling in northern Jordan. The wrong Mercedes was hit. The second came in 1972 with a strike by Super Mystères on a building in Qabatiya, Lebanon. Limited only to cannon, they perforated the second floor of the building but missed the quarry.
6. Dishon, *Middle East Record, Volume Four 1968*, p. 368. These were held to ensure Jordan returned the three dead left behind. The exchange occurred on 28 March with Israel getting three coffins, two of which were filled with sand and rocks. It appeared that the Jordanians had difficulty recovering anything of the badly burnt corpses.
7. Dishon, *Middle East Record, Volume Four 1968*, p. 367, gives an Israeli newspaper account recording mortar bombs, recoilless rifle fire and small arms rounds discouraging the operation. See also Trevor N. Dupuy, *Elusive Victory: The Arab-Israeli Wars 1947–1974* (Fairfax, Virginia: Hero Books, 1984), p. 353. Other sources suggest it was a diversion or are entirely silent about the Abdullah Bridge movement.
8. Sharon and Chanoff, *Warrior*, unpaginated (search for 'driven away.').
9. Arafat was featured on the cover of *Time Magazine* on 13 December 1968. Nasser brought Arafat to Moscow during his July 1968 visit to introduce the Palestinian to the Soviets and the USSR began supplying munitions in competition with China.
10. Avneri, *War of Attrition*, p. 127.
11. The IDF figure may represent only direct engagements and not standoff attacks or mines while the Fedayeen figure are only confirmed kills and does not include mortally-wounded fedayeen and those killed by air or artillery attack.
12. Avneri, *War of Attrition*, p. 147.
13. Aaron Yaffe, 'The War of Attrition in the "Land of Pursuits": The 1968–1970 War in the Jordan Valley', Ariel Center for Policy Research, <http://www.acpr.org.il/English/0907-YaffeE.pdf> accessed 5 April 2021, p. 1 and Samuel M. Katz, *Follow Me!, A History of Israel's Military Elite* (London, England: Arms and Armour Press, 1989), p. 97.
14. Roth, *The Air Force in the War of Attrition*, p. 53 and Avneri, *War of Attrition*, p. 138.

ABOUT THE AUTHOR

William J. Norton is retired from a flight test engineering career that spanned 40 years, including 20 as a US Air Force officer. He has held numerous positions in many organisations on dozens of aerospace programs spanning all aircraft types. He has penned scores of technical papers, 18 books, and a multitude of magazine articles. Bill holds a Masters in Aeronautical Engineering and has taught courses at the college-level. He is a civil pilot with numerous ratings, restored and operated a DHC-1 Chipmunk, and built a Rutan Long-EZ. Bill is married to the lovely and talented Anya Victoria Eriksson.